This book is comprised of five books (making it a $34.75 total value!) Your books are presented in this order:

1. The Ultimate Collection of Resurrections and Rebirths
2. The Ultimate Collection of Famous Virgin Births
3. The Absolutely Essential Tips for Buying & Selling On eBay
4. The Absolutely Essential Guide to Understanding Elder Financial Abuse
5. 100 Great Lines to Put in Your Personal Ad

I0471067

These books are sold and/or distributed with the understanding that the publishers and authors are not engaged in rendering legal or other professional services. **These books and its subject matter are for entertainment purposes only.** In this publication there may be inadvertent inaccuracies including technical inaccuracies, typographical inaccuracies and other possible inaccuracies. **The writers and publishers of these publications expressly disclaim all liability for the use or interpretation by anybody of information contained in these publications.** The authors, publishers and distributors of these publications hereby disclaim any and all liability for any loss or damage caused by errors or omissions resulted from negligence, accident, or any other causes. If legal advice or other expert assistance is required, the services of a competent professional person in a consultation capacity should be sought. Products, services and websites' content vary with time. Please verify any published information.

<u>Absolutely Essential Tips For Buying & Selling On eBay</u> - Special Edition - 5 Books in One

TABLE OF CONTENTS

Book #1 - The Ultimate Collection of Resurrections and Rebirths

Book #2 - The Ultimate Collection of Famous Virgin Births

Book #3 - Absolutely Essential Tips For Buying & Selling On eBay

Book #4 - The Absolutely Essential Guide to Understanding Elder Financial Abuse

Book #5 - **100 Great Lines to Put In Your Personal Ads**

The Ultimate Collection of Resurrections and Rebirths

As Christianity and Jesus Christ are central figures to the resurrection theme in western culture, let's first review Christianity before presenting the list of famous figures.

Christian History and Doctrine of the Universe

People often approach the history of Christianity as they do driving. They learn it once then assume they always know it. There's much about this religion which people either never knew or have forgotten. With that in mind, let's briefly recap the chronicle of Jesus, the early Christians and the Bible.

In 63 B.C., Roman General Pompey conquered Palestine.

After this bloody conquest, frustrated Hebrew priests began prophesying that a great spiritual leader would arise to liberate the battle weary Jewish people. Many declared themselves to be the messiah and began prophesying at markets and on street corners. Many "false Christs" sprang up. Some developed a following, most did not.

Jesus started his ministry after visiting, and being baptized by, the popular John the Baptist. John prophesied that Jesus was the messiah.

Jesus' ministry was successful, primarily on the strength of his reputation for doing miracles.

Against the advice of his disciples, Jesus went to Jerusalem and, tragically, was crucified outside the city. A few days later, probably in Galilee, his disciples and others, claimed Jesus had risen from the dead and urged them to continue spreading his word.

The first several generations of Christians were largely driven on by their fanatical certainty of an impending "Judgment Day." They needed to spread the word to as many people as possible and as fast as possible. This burning desire provided much needed drive. Jewish authorities proved uninterested in them and often hostile, so they began increasingly spreading the word to non-Jewish people in the surrounding provinces and beyond.

The first post-Jesus Christian leader was St. Peter, which is one reason why the pope is said to have "St. Peter's chair." Around 44 AD, it appears James, probably a relative of Jesus, became leader. These very early Christians were called "Jewish Christians" and still wholeheartedly considered themselves Jewish. That, however, was about to change. In 66 AD, the Jews revolted against Roman occupation. Though Jewish leaders asked for their aid in the revolt, the "Jewish Christians" refused and fled Jerusalem. The Jewish priests felt betrayed and became more hostile towards the new "Jewish Christians." The Jewish revolt was brutally crushed by 70 AD, but a serious rift had been created between the two religions.

The fleeing Jewish Christians were now in several places, and, unlike before, in mostly gentile areas. Their numbers were growing fast. They began being called just "Christian" instead of "Jewish Christian."

A good deal of this phenomenal Christian growth was due to the efforts of a man named Saul. We know him as St. Paul. Initially he hated Christians, torturing and probably killing several. But after having a dream or vision, he traveled a great deal, preaching the Christian word. Several of his letters to new, fledgling Christian churches are included in the New Testament.

St. Peter took his following to Rome and became the first Bishop of Rome. He held services where the Vatican is now.

Very difficult times lay ahead for early Christians. Many Christians and Jews wouldn't worship both their God and the gods of Rome. Rome considered this treasonous and atheistic. That changed in 312 A.D. when Roman Emperor Constantine had a dream or vision that if he rode with the sign of a cross into a coming battle, he would win. He did and won. Constantine then decreed tolerance for Christianity. (Please note that there are at least 64 Christian crosses.) The cross Constantine wore into battle didn't look anything like the cross as we know it. It was "Constantine's Cross". Also remember that Christianity didn't become the Roman empire's official religion until late in that century. Constantine in 312 only decreed "tolerance" for it. Constantine himself didn't get baptized until on his deathbed. In those days, and for by far the history of Christianity, you simply *weren't* Christian {except in special cases} unless you were baptized.)

We skip past the rigid Middle and Dark Ages, stopping at 1382. Few people could read enough to understand a book. Books and education were for the clergy and rich. Western Bibles were mostly in Greek or Latin, both being languages the common man knew little or nothing of. Though it may be hard to image, unlike today, Bibles were *rarely* ever read by Christians. They listened to the priest who told them what God wanted and that was that. An event in 1382 would change all this.

In that year, Englishman John Wycliffe and his followers, translated the first Bible into the English language. A revised version came out in 1388. Suddenly the scriptures were available to millions because Englishmen could read English, but not the church's official languages, Latin or Greek. New preachers sprang up and the Catholic Church, still firmly in command, became quite agitated. Archbishop Arundel (leader of Catholic England,) in 1412, spoke of Wycliffe in this way: *"that wretched and pestilent fellow of damnable memory...the very herald and child of anti-Christ, who crowned his wickedness by translating the scriptures into the mother tongue."* [4] A church council in the early 15th century decreed *"no one shall in the future translate on his own authority any text of holy scriptures into the English tongue--nor shall any man read this kind of book, booklet or treaties, now recently composed in the time of the said John Wycliffe or later, or any that shall be composed in future, in whole or part, publicly or secretly, under penalty of the greater excommunication."* (Back then, excommunication was considered a far greater penalty than it is now.) [5]

The first Bible to be printed by the revolutionary movable type printing press was the Gutenberg Bible. Q surviving Gutenberg Bible can be worth a million dollars. But the printing of these historical masterpieces left Mr. Gutenberg bankrupt. He died destitute. [6]

In 1611, the most influential English Bible came out, "The King James Version," from which most of the versions we have today originate. Bible readers might be interested to know that the wording in a Bible reflects the language of when it was translated into English, not when the New Testament originally was compiled, roughly 1800 years ago. For instance, Exodus 34:17 from the King James Version reads "Thou shalt make thee no molten Gods." This literally is how most English people, particularly the more academically inclined, spoke in the late 1500s and very early 1600's when the King James Version was written.

The New Testament and Its History

After Alexander the Great's conquest of the Eastern Mediterranean in 332 B.C., Greek became the dominate scholarly language of the Holy Lands. There exists no scientifically verifiable information as to what Jesus said during his lifetime. Thus, it's thought the first accounts of Jesus' life and teachings were oral. Since Greek was the area's "official" written language, the first written language of the New Testament, once compiled was Greek. Because Jesus was born a Hebrew and lived in the land of the Hebrews, the languages he and his followers spoke would have been Hebrew and/or its related language, Aramaic. Thus, Jesus had a Hebrew/Aramaic name at birth. That name is *Yehoshua*, or Yeshu for short. One rendering of Yehoshua is *Joshua*. The Greek *translation* of Yehoshua (Joshua) is Jesus. It's doubtful Jesus was ever called "Jesus" while alive. This is primarily because his followers were Hebrew and spoke Aramaic and Hebrew, not Greek. Years later, when Greek writers were writing and compiling the New Testament, they translated his Hebrew name of Yehoshua into the Greek name Jesus. It's probable that Jesus was also never called "Christ" while alive. Since he was Hebrew, and lived primarily in Hebrew lands, he most likely was called "Hammasiah" (Hebrew) or "Mesima" (Aramaic) by his followers. "Ho Christos" is the Greek translation of the Hebrew word mashiakh. It means "an anointed one." Over the years, "Ho Christos" was shortened to "Christ." The word "Bible" is the English translation of the Latin word for "books," "*biblia*." Thus, the term "Bible" wasn't a popular word until well after the 14th century when the Latin Bible was translated into English.

Archaeologists have discovered 20 partial or complete very early Christian gospels, though many are Gnostic (see glossary) in origin. The most significant of these new discoveries may be the Gospel of Thomas which was written before either of the four familiar gospels in the Bible. Nobody is sure why the four familiar gospels were chosen and how. In fact, three or more of these 20 recently discovered gospels or remnants of gospels are thought to be written before the four gospels in the Bible.

Perhaps you've heard the assertion that Luke was a doctor who traveled with St. Paul. Another claim is that Mark was a secretary of St. Peter. Confusing matters though is that there is *no* scientifically verifiable evidence for these legends. It appears much more likely that they're literally lore which was handed down from earlier Christian generations. In fact, there is great question as to whether the texts were written entirely by individuals. Collections of priests and worshipers probably wrote most or all of the gospels.

The Epistles are the oldest part of the New Testament and 1 Thessalonians is its oldest book dating back to around 49 A.D. The earliest of the four traditional gospels is Mark. It was written between 65 and 70 A.D. This gospel apparently originated in Rome where the writer or writers were urging on the terribly persecuted Christians. Roman emperor and first class psychopath, Nero, had blamed the Christians for Rome's gigantic fire of 64 A.D. Terrible persecutions of Christians resulted.

Around 85-95 A.D., the Gospel of Luke appeared, probably to convince authority that Christianity was the new Judaism and should be treated better. The Gospel of Matthew was written around 90 A.D. Its primary function was to provide a compilation of Jesus' work. The Gospel of John was written around 100-110 A.D. and is intended to deny the interpretation of Jesus work by the "heretical" Gnostics and others.

The first "heretics" in Christian history actually speeded up the compilation of the New Testament. This "alternative approach" Christianity was preached by the Gnostics (not related to the agnostics.)

There were Jewish Gnostics and Christian Gnostics. The branch of Christianity which survives and prospers today, though, was primarily concerned with it's fast growing competition, the Christian Gnostics. (*Around the middle of the 2nd century, roughly 25 to 35% of all Christians were Gnostic.*) These followers of Christ felt that everything on earth is evil and the only salvation for man is for his soul to reach heaven. As part of its extreme fatalism, procreation, marriage and birth were abhorred. Orthodox Gnostics even felt being female was a curse as females physically brought us low life humans into this dark, miserable world. They were quite anti-Semitic and had a difficult time using the Jewish Bible (the Christian Old Testament) so one of their leaders, Marcion, in 140 A.D., collected a number of very early Christian writings, making changes in the text where he saw fit, put them together and formed a smaller "New Testament. (They were the first to use the term "New Testament.") This Gnostic competition, and the enormous growth both branches of Christianity were experiencing, gave the non-Gnostic Christians incentive to speed up work on their own New Testament.

A great number of discrepancies between New Testament manuscripts have been found. One Biblical scholar in 1707 estimated there were around 30,000. Generally the discrepancies are very minor. One which may not be deals with Mark 6:3. This verse describes Jesus as "the carpenter, son of Mary." However, Origen (died 254 A.D.,) one of the best Biblical scholars of his time, claims he never saw a manuscript which read "carpenter" but saw instead Jesus was "the son of a carpenter." *(Most modern day Bible scholars think that due largely to where Jesus lived much of his early adult life, he did what around half the people did in that area which was working in stone quarries and/or being a stone mason. Few Biblical scholar still think he was a carpenter.)* Another deals with the inspirational parables of the adulteress brought to Jesus for punishment (John 8:1-11.) It doesn't appear in any early texts Biblical scholars are aware of. It does have the character of Jesus so its addition to the New Testament is well accepted.

By 180 A.D., the New Testament was mostly written and compiled. At present, the Bible has been at least partially translated into more than 1,200 languages. A count taken in 1977 found 36 English versions of the Bible and 1399 non-English versions.

Classical Christian Doctrines about God and the Universe

Now that we have reviewed its history, let's continue by briefly summarizing classical Christian doctrines about God and the universe.

1. God has always existed and always will. He has absolute knowledge of the past, present, and the future--and lives in a place called heaven where he rules the universe. In heaven are many angels and the souls of good people that God has allowed to enter its gates.

2. Many years in the past, God created an angel named Lucifer. Lucifer was blessed with great beauty. His job was to guard God's throne. Lucifer was the second most powerful force in the entire universe.

3. Lucifer, however, had higher ambitions than just being the second most powerful force in the universe. Motivated by greed and a big ego, Lucifer decided to reject the laws of God and try a coup in heaven. He gathered a number of angels as supporters and they tried to overthrow God but were unsuccessful. God threw Lucifer out of heaven, along with the other angels who supported him.

4. God decided to punish Lucifer and the fallen angels, so he created a lake of eternal fire to torment them and anyone else who, in the future, might choose to rebel. We know this "lake of fire" as "hell." Lucifer, (whose name then changed to Satan,) and the other "misguided" angels will get cast into hell on the great Judgment Day, which has yet to come.

5. God created man and placed him in the Garden of Eden. God created much animal and plant life for the garden. God gave the first two people he created, Adam and Eve, everything they could possibly want in life. God gave Adam and Eve free choice to serve him or to reject him as their Lord. God made it clear he would continue to provide for them as long as the first couple followed his laws. To test Adam and Eve and their offspring, should they bear children, God created within the Garden of Eden a tree from which he commanded them not to eat. God told them that if they eat the fruit from that special tree, they would die, both spiritually and physically.

6. Satan found out about this. He wanted man to sin. He wanted man to rebel against God as he did. Satan, in the form of a snake, approached Eve and told her that the tree which God had declared off-limits bore the Garden's best fruit. At first Eve refused to listen to Satan but later tried the

fruit anyway. Eve also talked Adam into eating the apple. They now had sinned against the word of God. God knew this had happened. He came to the Garden and in a rage threw them out. As continued punishment, he gave to women terrible pain during childbirth. As punishment to man, he said that man must work all the days of his life.

7. Because of Adam and Eve's sin (known as "Original Sin,") all of humanity was condemned. In his continued rage, God promised to punish all future humans by sending them to the lake of fire (hell) after death even if they had been good all their lives. Mankind was powerless to do anything but accept its terrible fate.

8. *Thousands of years later*, God decided to take pity on his human creation. He sent his only son, Jesus Christ, to give man a second chance to get into heaven. God impregnated Jesus' mother Mary in a manner which kept her virginity intact. God said that the blood Jesus shed on the cross would be enough for mankind to atone for its sins and thus be allowed in heaven after which individual souls would regain their original sinless status.

9. However, God said that for people to take advantage of this unusual and special outpouring of love by their Creator, they must personally request it by accepting Jesus and his teachings. This includes asking God to forgive them for their own sins and their ancestor's sins (Adam and Eve's "Original Sin" and any sins their direct ancestors made for the last three or four generations.) After individuals do that, God will pardon them, thus making it possible for the converted to go to heaven after death and stay for eternity.

10. Those who reject the Son of God as their Savior, those who belong to most other religions, those who didn't know of this option for salvation and those who don't take any position one way or the other, will not be pardoned for the "Original Sin," their past family's sins and their own sins and thus will be cast in the lake of fire, tormented forever. (This position would centuries later be amended to include the Hebrew Patriarchs of the Old Testament, babies that died before baptism and the handicapped.)

Deserving special attention is the paragraph in which God in his fury sent almost everybody to hell from the time of Adam and Eve to the time of Jesus' ministry. Thus, if you use the Biblical time frame to determine the number of years mankind has existed (around 6,000), *all humans went to hell, no matter what, for around 4,000 years.* (Again this position would be amended centuries later to include around 1 or 2% of mankind's population.)   This includes all the ancient Greeks, all the ancient Egyptians, etc.   Of course, you can't go to heaven through any other religion (besides Judaism depending on what part of the world and what century you were living in) *only hell*.   The third of the four classical Christian spiritual laws states that.   Taking Jesus as your Lord and Savior is the *only* way into heaven, no ifs, ands or buts.   This is a doctrine which remains very strong today.   Since so many *billions* of people in the history of mankind haven't been saved and/or have worshipped in other religions, they've been condemned, according to literal Christian scripture, to hell. Hell should have billions of souls in it by now, at least.

There were many very influential and even extremely popular gods, prophets and other "divine" people from other religions worshipped in the Roman Empire in the years prior to the writing of the New Testament and/or during the time of its writing, who, as encyclopedias and scholars tell us, also were "resurrected"

It is important to remember that during the time period that the New Testament was being written and compiled, in Rome, the Greek and Roman gods, as well as Mithra were *much* more popular than Jesus.

The dying-and-rising god (also known as a death-rebirth-deity) is part of many older cultures and civilizations. A dying-and-rising god refers to a deity which returns by being reborn or resurrected, in either a symbolic or literal sense.

Famous Resurrected People and Deities

The following is a list of historically famous resurrected people and deities from tradition, mythology and other text. There may be more than one version of events for some of the below that is not presented.

Please note that not everybody agrees as to their resurrection/rebirth and presented specifics. Further research on each of the following is advocated before making a definitive statement as to its regard.

(In regard to an entry with a question mark after them, I was not able to get adequate confirmation information. You however might be able to.)

ADONIS - (Greece) (**1**) Venus saw him hunting and fell in love with him. This offended Mars, the rival for the affections of Venus, and he assumed the form of a wild boar and killed Adonis who was hunting. Venus mourned exceedingly. She was so overcome with grief and fear that she went down into the lower regions (underworld) to bring back her lover (Adonis). But Pluto's wife saw how handsome Adonis was and she would not let him go back up to earth with Venus so they came to an agreement where they would divide the year into halves, and each in turn should have him for a half. (**2**) A very handsome boy who Zeus was persuaded by the goddess Aphrodite to resurrect each year for 6 months.

AENEAS – (Rome) – According to the ancient writer Virgil, Aeneas is devastated by Troy being ruined. Aeneas dies (goes to the underworld) and comes back as a new, determined more optimistic Aeneas.

ATUNIS – See the Greek God *Adonis*.

ALCESTIS - When it came time for the Greek deity Admetus to die, Apollo arraigned for someone else to die for him. The deity Alcestis volunteers and died for him, but is resurrected after other gods decided that such an arrangement was unethical.

ASSUR - Assur is thought to be the pre-Egyptian king and conqueror of a huge amount of the ancient world, including what would become Egypt.

UrRea was an agrarian civilization in the Nile Delta before there was an Egypt. Storytellers handed down the history of that period for countless generations before there was writing.

We're told that Assur cleared jungles, drained swamps and dug canals. He determined which plants were fit for food and medicine. He taught his people agriculture and animal husbandry. He started the first kingdom, made laws, taught people to worship the gods and even ended cannibalism. After he had raised his own people up from savagery, he went about civilizing the whole world.

Assur's wife was the legendary Isis. One day the evil god Set, and other conspirators killed Assur. They cut his body into pieces and scattered his severed parts in many places.

Assur's faithful wife Isis gathered his scattered body parts and put them all back together. She also resurrected Assur from the dead. After his resurrection, they had a son, Heru. Assur would become the king of the afterlife and judge of the dead. Isis went on to become the EarthMother Goddess. (Isis thus could be considered the original Eve.) Heru went on to become the progenitor of all the Pharaohs and the patriarch of Egyptian civilization. Set went on to become Satan, the god of evil of the Egyptian religion. All the Pharaohs traced their lineage to the gods, Assur, Isis, and Heru.

Note: The people of UrRea were UrReans, not Africans. They spoke UrRean languages, not Egyptian. They didn't become Egyptians until after the birth of Isis and the resurrection of Assur. This pre-Egyptian UrRean civilization in the Nile Delta was related to Pre-Sumerian and Pre-Akkadian civilizations between the Tigris and Euphrates rivers.

Assur is known as "Osiris" in conventional mythology. The ancient Greeks translated his name to be that. When Alexander the Great conquered Egypt, that land was called "Mis-Ur-Re" thus Egypt was called *Mis-Ur-Re* before it was called Egypt. The Greeks changed the name of the country to "Egyptos". Then they gave the Egyptian gods Greek names. Osiris was Assur for thousands of years before he was called Osiris. Heru's name would be translated by the Greeks into "Horus".

ATTIS - A Mesopotamian (Phrygian) god. He sacrificed himself to Zeus (called Jupiter by the Roman Priests,) but is resurrected every spring.

BAAL – Baal (or Ba'al) means "master" or "lord". Many deities in various parts of the world were called Baal (or Ba'al). Ba'al of Tyre is Melqart. See *Melqart*. In this version of events, Baal goes down to the underworld and dies. In a vision the chief god, El, sees that Baal has returned to life and Baal returns to his throne.

BACCHUS - The Roman god of wine and intoxication. It's Greek equivalent is Dionysus. See *Dionysus*.

BALDR (also Balder, Baldur) – A famous figure in old Norse/Danish poetry. One account has Baldr mistakenly dying from the arrow, (another account has it as a spear) of his blind brother Barbarika. His death led to the destruction of the gods at Ragnarök and according to Völuspá, Baldr will be reborn in the new world.

BARI – (Korea) - This is a myth regarding the origin of the shamans. The ancestral shaman is believed to be Bari, a sacred woman. She works many miracles. She goes down into the underworld (where the dead go) and not only frees people from it but returns to life up here. Her royal parents die and she brings them back to life. Bari became the death goddess, the guider of the dead to the Underworld. She also became the first shaman, and the patron of all the shamans in Korea.

BUDDIAH (Siddhartha Gautama) - He along with Horus, Mithra, Dionysus and Osiris have the most glaring similarities to Jesus' life as we know it. Buddha was born to the Virgin Maya on December 25th. (Not all agree on this date of birth.) His birth was announced by a star in the sky and his birth drew wise men presenting costly gifts. He was baptized in water. Buddha healed the sick and fed 500 from a small basket of cakes and even walked on water. He died (on a cross, in some traditions,) was buried but arose again after his tomb was opened by supernatural powers. He ascended into heaven but is expected to return in later days to judge the dead and certain others. As noted, Buddiah was resurrected when his tomb was opened by supernatural powers.

CASTOR & POLLUX - Sons of Zeus though some accounts have them as mortals. When Castor was killed, Zeus was quite unhappy and decided to have each son live on alternating days. Pollux is given two options by Zeus and this is the one he chose.

CHINNAMASTA - (Northern India and Nepal) - Translated to be "She whose head is severed". Chhinnamasta is recognized by both Buddhists and Hindus. She's equated with Chinnamunda – the severed-headed form of the Tibetan Buddhist goddess Vajrayogini. Her head was cut off and she came back to life (or never died) and lived on. Among other things she is the goddess of sexual desire.

DIONYSOS - (Greece) - This is a Phrygian and later adopted Greek god. He along with Horus, Mithra, Buddha, Krishna and Osiris have the most glaring similarities to Jesus' life as we know it. He was born of a Virgin on December 25th or January 6th. (December 25th would be the date the ancient

Greeks would settle on.) He was placed in a manger. (Mangers were a lot more of a commonplace in those days since there were so many horses. Mangers were where many poorer travelers were allowed to stay.) He was a traveling teacher who performed many miracles. He turned water into wine. His followers could eat a sacred meal. He is said to have rose from the dead on March 25th. He was called the "Redeemer," "Sin bearer," "King of Kings," "the Anointed One," "Only Begotten Son," "Savior."

DUMUZI - Tammuz was established in honor of the eponymous god Tammuz, who originated as a Sumerian shepherd-god, Dumuzid or Dumuzi. See *Tammuz*.

ESHMUN - (or Eshmoun, less accurately Esmun or Esmoun) – Eshmun was a Phoenician god of healing and the guardian or protector god of Sidon. The goddess Astronoë so harassed him with her love for him that in desperation he castrated himself and died. Astronoë resurrected him from the warmth of her body, and changed him into a god.

EURIDICE - (Greek) When Orpheus' wife Euridice dies of a snake bite, the grieving Orpheus went down to Hades (where all dead Greeks went according to tradition) and persuaded the god in charge, Pluto, to resurrect Euridice. Pluto promises to resurrect Eurydice if Orpheus doesn't look back at her as Orpheus heads back to earth, but he does and she doesn't make it past the underworld.

FRODE - Frode is the name of a number of legendary Danish kings including Beowulf. One version has a Frode disappearing into the earth for three years after he dies and then returning.

GULLVEIG - In Norse mythology, Gullveig is a speared, then burned three times. He however keeps getting reborn after each burning.

HAY-TAU - Egyptian vegetation god. He died and miraculously came back to life (with no other god's help) several years later.

HEITSI-EIBIB - (Saan, or Bushmen of Southern Africa) - Heitsi-eibib is said to have died and resurrected himself on several occasions. Because from this his funeral cairns (man-made pile [or stack] of stones) are found in many locations in southern Africa and it is customary to throw (or put) a stone onto them for good luck.

INANNA - The Sumerian goddess of sexual love, fertility, and warfare. She is the equivalent of the better known *Ishtar*. Inanna is reborn after she travels to the underworld and dies there. She descended into the land of the dead (underworld) which was ruled by her sister, Ereskeigal, the goddess of death and infertility. She went down there to rescue her lover, a vegetation god named Tammuz, who was being held hostage. In this version of events she is brought back to life when her servant sprinkled her with the "water of life."

IRAVAN – (South India) - (aka Aravan, Iravat and Iravant) - He is a character from the Hindu epic Mahabharata. One version is that the great Krishna allows Iravan to witness the entire duration of the Mahabharata war through the eyes of his severed head.

ISHTAR - East Semitic Akkadian, Assyrian and Babylonian goddess. In earlier Sumerian culture she was known as Inanna. See *Inanna*.

IZANAMI - (Izanami-no-kami and/or Izanagi no Mikoto) – (Japan) - ?

JESUS CHRIST – Jesus was resurrected.

JARILO – (Yarilo, Iarilo, or Gerovit) – (Slavic) – Jarilo is believed to be (re)born and killed every year. His mythical life cycle followed the yearly life of various types of vegatation.

KOSTROMA - (Slavic) – ?

KRISHNA - (Chrishna) - The mother of Chrishna (Devaki) was "overshadowed" (taken sexually) by the supreme god, Brahma. Chrishna's mother had given birth seven times before but still remained a virgin (as was the case with Mother Mary who gave birth to 3 boys, including Jesus, and also still remained a virgin.) Krishna's birth was announced by a star. Krishna was born in a cave, which at the time of his birth was miraculously illuminated. King Kansa sought the life of the Indian Christ by ordering the massacre of all male children born during the same night as Krishna. Krishna traveled widely, performing miracles, including raising the dead, healing lepers, healing the blind and the deaf. The crucified Krishna is pictured on the cross with arms extended. Pierced by an arrow while hanging on the cross, Krishna died, but descended into Hell from which He rose again on the third day and ascended into Heaven. (The Gospel of Nicodemus tells of Jesus' descent into Hell.) He is expected to return on the last day. Chrishna's birthday is often thought to be December 25th. (Others claim that Krishna's birth was in July, August or September.)

LEMMINKÄINEN - Lemminkäinen is a prominent figure in Finnish mythology. He is one of the Heroes of the Kalevala. Lemminkäinen dies and in an effort to reassemble him, his mother searches all over for all parts of his body. Finally, with help, she is able to get him to live again.

MARZANNA – (Mara, Maržena, Morana, Moréna, Mora or Marmora) - Slavic goddess associated with death and rebirth of nature including seasonal agricultural growth and death.

MELQART – (Melqart-Heracles, Herakles) – Melqart's Greek equivalent is Heracles) - This Phoenician god is resurrected. Melqart is respected and/or worshiped in Phoenician and Punic cultures from Syria to Spain. He is the god of the Phoenician city of Tyre. Heracles was killed by a Typhon and raised from the dead by Iolaos.

MITHRA - "Christianity's sister religion." He along with Horus, Osiris, Krishna, Dionysus and Buddha have the most glaring similarities to Jesus' life as we know it. Mithra had a virgin birth of a sort, Mithra was said to be born from the "rock of a cave" while shepherds and many Magi looked on.

Mithra came to be known as the all important sun God. He originally was a Zoroastrian God who people began to associate independently of Zoroastrianism. *Mithraism is often called Christianity's "sister religion" largely because there are so many similarities between the two and it originated and was popular prior to Christianity.* Mithraism spread into Greek and Roman influenced areas from Persia, coming to Rome in 68 B.C. It, and the worship of Greek and Roman Gods, were Christianity's biggest competition until the latter 3rd century. In fact, until the latter 3rd century, it was a more popular religion than Christianity.

Many of Mithraism's doctrines are strikingly similar to Christianity. In particular, communion, the use of holy water, the adoration of shepherds at Mithras' birth, the use of Sundays for the Sabbath instead of the traditional Saturday which is the Sabbath of the Jewish people, and using the date of December 25th as the birth date of both Jesus and Mithra, (it had been celebrated as Mithra's birth date for many years before Christians adopted it for Jesus.) Also the Mithraic belief in the immortality of the soul, the last judgment and the resurrection preceded Christianity's adopting those beliefs. However, it's different from Christianity in significant ways also. Mithra was considered a God not a prophet. Its secretive ceremonies excluded women. They also had other lesser gods.

Mithraism was quite popular with Roman soldiers. Though it preached brotherly love, as with Islam and Sikhism, it wished to aid the soldier in battle. People becoming Mithraistic were often baptized in the blood of a bull. After Christianity became Rome's official religion, Christians destroyed most of the Mithratic temples and killed any Mithratic clergy they could find.

Mithraism exposed millions of people to doctrines and procedures which would later be preached by the newcomer, Christianity. Its similarities with Christianity may have made it easier for Christian doctrines to have been so quickly and readily accepted. Had Christianity not been so successful, it's possible Mithraism would have become the official religion of Rome.

Mithra was resurrected after death but he comes back as another person.

ODIN – (Norse Mythology) – Odin is a major Norse god and was popular with the Vikings. Odin lost an eye. His love for wisdom however was so strong that he was willing to sacrifice his life to try and find more knowledge of the world. He gained insight by hanging himself for nine days from Yggdrasil, the cosmic tree. Following his voluntary death he had a magical resurrection.

OBATALA - (Yoruba people) - Obatala is a dying and rising god. He left his Temple on the seventh day of the Itapa festival, stayed in his grave on the eighth day and returned in a great procession to his Temple on the ninth day.

ORION – Associated with Osiris. See *Osiris*.

ORPHEUS - Orpheus was a legendary poet, prophet and musician in ancient Greek religion and myth. In his quest to get his wife Eurydice reborn after her untimely death, he was one of the handful of Greek heroes to visit the Underworld and returned alive (thus he didn't so much die but went to the underworld and returned alive.)

OSIRIS - The Egyptian god who was murdered and resurrected. He however was resurrected only in the after world, thus becoming the very important Egyptian god (and king) of the afterlife. See "*Assur*". "Osiris" was the translated name given to Assur" by the Greeks who in many ways adopted Assur.

OUROBOROS - An ancient symbol showing a serpent or dragon eating its own tail. It is a symbol of resurrection.

PERSEPHONE - Persephone was abducted by Hades the god-king of the Greek underworld. She would become his wife making her the queen of the underworld. Because Persephone had tasted of the food of Hades she was forced to forever spend a part of the year with her husband in the underworld. Her annual return to the earth was in the spring and that made her the Goddess of spring. Her return to the underworld in winter, conversely was associated with the dying of plants until she returned to the upper world in spring.

PHOENIX - A phoenix obtains new life by arising from the ashes of its predecessor.

PROSERPINA – (Proserpina, Proserpine, Persephone) – She is an ancient Roman goddess whose story is the basis of a myth of springtime. Her Greek goddess equivalent is Persephone. Pluto, Roman king of the underworld, came out of the underworld and abducted her to live with him down in the underworld. She would eventually be freed but would have to live three months of each year with Pluto, and stay the rest with her mother who wasn't in the underworld.

QUETZALCOATL - Quetzalcoatl was born of a virgin around 900 BC. His story is told by the Aztecs and Mayans. He was crucified (or sets himself on fire after over-drinking depending on the version.) He was considered the God of light that struggled against the god of darkness called Tezcatlipoca. He was associated with the planet Venus, the morning star, like Jesus is. The cross was used as a symbolic representation. He said he would return from the dead to claim his earthly kingdom.

RA - Ra was identified primarily with the sun and is a major god in the religion of ancient Egypt. Humans were created from Ra's tears and sweat. Ra would go to the underworld at night (which is largely why it got dark) and be is reborn ddaily for the sun to rise.

TAMMUZ - (Arabic) - An ancient Sumerian-Akkadian god who dies and is resurrected every year. Many religious historians consider him the great grand daddy of all religious resurrections. The Sumerians are thought to have worshipped him (and his resurrection) as far back as 4,000 BC. (2) His Greek equivalent is "Adonis". See *Adonis*.

XIPE TOTEC – The Aztec god of rebirth and more. He doesn't get reborn as such, he flays his skin regularly and it grows back with no problem.

ZALMOXIS – Zalmoxis is another Life-Death-Rebirth deity. Some see him as a figure that resurrects.

ZOROASTRIANISM - While it currently has only an estimated 250,000 believers (1990 statistic), primarily in India and Iran, this religion and it's offshoot religion, Mithraism, has had a tremendous impact on the development of Christianity and Judaism.

Founded by the Persian prophet Zoroaster sometime between 1000 and 600 B.C., it's one of the world's original *dualistic* religions (see glossary for definition of dualism). It was practiced most by people in Arabia, and south-central Asia. Verifiable history shows it flourishing in the Persian Empire by 550 B.C.

After Alexander the Great's invasion of Persia (334 B.C.,) Zoroastrianism lost most of its followers. It wouldn't experience a serious revival until hundreds of years later. Zoroastrianism once again lost popularity when in roughly 637 A.D., Islamic forces conquered much of the territory it was practiced in, forcibly replacing it with Islam.

Like Christianity, Zoroastrianism is dualistic. It preaches that there is a struggle between good and evil forces for mastery of the universe. The good God and creator of the universe, is Ahura Mazda. The evil demon is Ahriman and he's bent on destroying everything good in the universe.

Zoroaster was sent down by God (Ahura Mazda) to help humans fight evil. He received the sacred laws of God, the Avesta on Mount Sabalan, in Persia. If an individual were to choose the path of goodness which Zoroaster represents, then on Judgment Day, he/she would go to heaven. At some point, a great battle between God, his angels (the "Amesha Spenta") and those "good" converted humans will occur against the evil demons and "bad" people who have not "converted." This will be the final battle and be the final "Judgment of the Dead." *Since this was preached, at least in Jesus' area, six to ten centuries before Jesus was even born, it's history's original "Judgment Day."* Peace will reign on earth after this battle because it is now cleansed of evil (unlike the Christian version of Judgment Day which assumes it is the end of the world.)

Many similarities exist between Zoroastrianism, Judaism and Christianity. Both Zoroaster and Moses got their respective religious "Laws" from their one true God on a mountain (he getting the Avesta from Ahura Mazda on Mt. Sabalan and Moses getting the Judaic "laws" from Yahweh on Mt. Sinai.) Each is dualistically fighting a power of evil, Ahura Mazda against Ahriman, and Yahweh and the God of Christianity against Satan. The Zoroastrian all important first period of creation is divided into 6 parts as the Old Testament account of creation is divided into six days. A human couple is the first human beings for each religion,

Moshya and Moshyana by the Zoroastrian account and Adam and Eve by the other two religious accounts. A terrible winter was sent by Ahura Mazda, as told in the Avesta, to punish mankind for its evil. This, of course, parallels the great flood theory. All three religions believes in a good life after death for the righteous and a hellish life after death for the unrighteous. A Zoroastrian, during a religious ceremony, drinks milk and water and eats bread. Originally, Christians did the same with wine and unleavened bread (now it's more often wafer.) Zoroastrians celebrated high and low masses. A religion worshipping the lesser Zoroastrian God of light, Mithra, spread from Persia to the Mediterranean and even Rome. In fact, in Rome, it was a more popular religion than Christianity for almost the first three centuries A. D. Various Christian assertions including the date of December 25th for the traditional birthday of Jesus, comes from Mithraism (Mithra's birthday was celebrated on December 25th for many years prior to Jesus' birth.) For more information on what's called *Christianity's sister religion*, see the description of Mithraism in this section.

Afterlife from the Standpoint of Science

There are at least four, possibly five types of scientifically proven afterlife scenarios.

1) First off, genetics. When you procreate, a large portion of your DNA survives you in the form of your children, direct relatives and to a certain extent, your fellow human beings. If you have the DNA which make men lose their hair, that DNA is passed on and will probably be noticeable in generations preceding you. This is true, of course, about many physical, emotional and mental characteristics, and even diseases such as diabetes. People might be surprised how long an afterlife (at least physically) we have thanks to our DNA. Even though your son may not look or seem anything like your great, great, great, great, grandfather, present in your son's body is some of his DNA.

Scientists say we all come from a few original human beings. You may say this supports the theory of Creation but from a scientific standpoint it doesn't. First off, the earliest man-like creatures may have been asexual, being able to procreate all by themselves. (Sometimes referred to as hermaphrodites.) [6] This simply was a bad idea from the standpoint of evolution for the same reason that it is not a good idea for most relatives to procreate. Everybody's chromosome chains have weak links. Family members often have the same weak links. These weak links need to be substituted with stronger links. These stronger links are best supplied by a totally different family tree. Asexuality, while convenient, possibly would have doomed our species to countless mutations and unstable life forms.

2) Another form of afterlife is one's posthumous impact on other people. This impact doesn't have to be mankind as a whole but could be on a much smaller "group of people" such as one's family. If the family is still talking about your great, great, great grandmother, even occasionally, she would qualify for this type of "afterlife." It can be said then that Jesus has had a phenomenal afterlife. Others with impressive, though less spectacular afterlives include Alexander the Great, Abraham Lincoln and Galileo.

3) Nuclear physics tells us that our body's matter (atoms and molecules,) also has an afterlife. As an example, a dead body buried in the ground eventually provides nourishment for countless organisms, mostly microscopic. Perhaps a part of one's body is used in an organ transplant. This lies in the realm of physics known as Matter Transference.

4) Still a fourth type deals with Cryonics. The freezing of the body until another time in the future when it can be thawed out and reborn.

5) There are those who feel if you stop breathing, and/or your heart stops beating, but you are brought back to life via mouth to mouth resuscitation, CPR or the like, you have been "resurrected" and technically are living in an afterlife.

Epilogue

There are rare documented cases of the return to life of the clinically dead. This is known as Lazarus syndrome, a term originating from the Biblical story of the Resurrection of Lazarus.

Many who have had Near Death Experiences (NDE) have, in their opinion at least, seen and/or in some other way experienced the afterlife. If nothing else this type of experience makes many feel more at peace with the prospect of dying.

The Ultimate Collection of Famous Virgin Births

There were many very influential and popular gods, prophets and other "divine" people worldwide that were purported to have had "virgin (or miraculous) births" prior to the birth of Christ. This book has a huge list of them with accompanying details.

Virgin birth in humans is typically defined as a woman giving birth without the involvement of a male in the act of conception. She should have an intact hymen after the impregnation. In many cases the term *miraculous birth* is used interchangeably with *virgin birth* as the woman is impregnated in a manner that does not break her hymen. (Some "miraculous births" could better be described as "miraculous arrivals to earth.")

Mythology tells us that a male god might take some physical (possibly human) form and impregnating a woman, either through actual intercourse or by some other physical activity. That often gets included in the "virgin birth" category. Still this might not be considered true virgin birth by many as it might involve sexual reproductive activity of some sort, even intercourse! In contrast, the God of Christianity is not an anatomic male and does not have sexual relations of any sort with the Virgin Mary. In other words there is no sex. That argument is used often by Christen theologians to help make Jesus stands out. Islam also teaches that Mother Mary was a virgin when she conceived the Messiah. Various accounts still have Mother Mary being called a virgin after she had not only given birth to Jesus but also to Jesus' brothers James and John. (The same is said of Buddha's mother who had other children.)

Immaculate Conception is a dogma of the Catholic Church. It states that at the moment when Mary, Mother of Jesus Christ, was conceived in the womb of her mother, Mary was kept free of original sin by the power of God. Immaculately conceived however has also been used to note a virgin birth, specifically when the child came into being without a father or a biological equivalent.

By 1000 BC, the virgin birth tradition seems to gained steam, so much so that some biographies of kings and important men insist that they were not only divinely born, but said to have transcended death to become gods themselves.

In ancient Babylon, "virgin-births" were often the responsibility of the Ishtar priestesses. They conducted fertility rites, prophesied and performed elaborate rituals in Babylonian temples and other holy places. Along with that, the priestesses had a successful prostitution business which provided financial support for various temple activities.

Upon their return to Palestine, formerly enslaved Hebrews from Babylon brought back to the Mediterranean peoples wondrous tales of the priestesses and their blasphemous sexual ministries. Word about them spread.

The Ishtar priestess' roles were to be both mother to the prospective holy child and minister to the child's divine needs. "Holy Virgin" was the title of harlot-priestesses of Ishtar. The title didn't mean physical virginity, it simply meant "unmarried."

The Hebrews called those children of the priestesses "Bathur" which literally meant "virgin-born". The Hellenic (Greek dominated) world had no equivalent to the seemingly bizarre rituals of Ishtar and mistranslated and misunderstood the Hebrew's name "Bathur". They called it "Parthenioi", meaning "virgin-born" in Greek, but virginity in the sense of physical, not spiritual.

Some of the early leaders of The Church of Jesus Christ of Latter-day Saints (the largest of the Mormon denominations) taught that YEHOVAH (God) can have (or has) a physical body and that he came down to earth, had sexual intercourse with Mary and conceived the Messiah. This however was never made an official church doctrine and is rarely heard today.

A related definition of interest may be *Parthenogenesis*: when eggs develop into embryos without being fertilized by sperm. This occurs in some insects and reptiles. Could this be how human virgin births occur? Not likely according to scientists. On rare occasions human eggs do develop parthenogenetically, but the resulting embryo either dies or turns into an ovarian tumor.

During various time periods in Greece, it became so common for women to claim that a god had impregnated them, that those women were not often believed. At one point a reigning king supposedly issued an edict decreeing the death of all women who should "offer such an insult to deities" as to claim being impregnated by any of them.

Note 1: Hebrew teachings do not specify that their predicted Messiah would be of virgin birth.

Note 2: The Qur'an and other Islamic text note a number of miraculous births of biblical characters.

Note 3: The healing cult of Asclepius held that women could be impregnated with supernatural assistance.

Note 4: Offspring from unions between male gods and human females can be known as demigods.

Note 5: Virgin births were also claimed for many Egyptian pharaohs and others.

Note 6: Virgin births in the world of reptiles, insects and non-human animals is not a rare occurrence.

Below are gods, prophets and other important characters from religious and other text that are noted as being conceived from virgin and/or miraculous birth.

Even if the information following the name is not specific in regard to the purported virgin birth, information was previously obtained as to the claim's likely authenticity.

(Please note that not everybody agrees as to their divine birth and presented specifics. Further research on each of the following is advocated before making a definitive statement as to its regard.)

In regard to those entries with a question mark after them, I was not able to get adequate confirmation information. You however might be able to.

ALCIDES - His mother Alcmene is thought to have been a virgin even after his birth.

ADONIS - In Greek mythology, Adonis is the god of beauty and desire. He's an important figure in several mystery religions. Adonis was also resurrected after being killed by a wild boar.

AGDISTIS - One version of Agdistis' birth is that as the Great Mother (Gaia) slept, Zeus the great Greek supergod impregnated her.

ALEXANDER THE GREAT – Posthumously some began asserting that he was fathered by a serpent god. Another version has him the son of the king Philip's wife Olympias (Alexander's biological mother anyway), and the god Zeus. He was conceived by one of Zeus' thunderbolts. While alive he purportedly travelled to the Oasis of Amen so that he might be recognized as the god's son and thus become a legitimate and recognized king of Egypt. Here is a case where because of a man's great success many people thought it implied a divine origin.
ANTIOPE – (Ancient Greece) - ?

APHRODITE - Aphrodite is the Greek goddess of pleasure, love, procreation and beauty. Her Roman equivalent is the goddess Venus. According to Hesiod's Theogony, she was born when Cronus cut off Uranus's genitals and tossed them into the sea. She would rise from the sea foam. However, according to Homer's Iliad, she is the daughter of Zeus and Dione.

APOLLO – Father is Zeus, mother is Leto. There are conflicting reports as to his miraculous/virgin birth.

APOLLONIUS OF TYANA - He was a very popular 1st-century orator and philosopher around the time of Christ. He became known for his wisdom and magical powers. Documents claim he did basically the same things as Jesus did. Christians in the 4th century even compared him with Jesus. One account gives him a virgin birth. There have been those in the past that thought maybe he was Jesus.

APOLLONIUS OF CAPPADOCIA - Apollonius, The mother of Apollonius of Cappadocia, was impregnated by the supreme God Proteus.

ARION – Immaculately conceived by the Gods in the citadel of Byrsa.

AVATARS OF THE GOD - In Hinduism, Avatars of the god when living in the human realm, can and do slip into human women's wombs without intercourse.

ASCLEPIUS – He was created when the Greek god Apollo mated with the mortal Coronis. He is the Greek patron of medicine. Among other things, he can/could heal the sick and bring the dead back to life.

ATHENA – Athena is the goddess of wisdom, inspiration, courage, law and justice, civilization, just warfare, mathematics, strength, the arts, crafts, strategy and skill. Athena is also a good friend of heroes and was the goddess of heroic endeavor and war strategies. She also is the virgin patroness of Athens, Greece.

Athena is thought to never had a lover and thus is known as "Athena Parthenos", "Virgin Athena". Her most famous temple is the Parthenon, on the Acropolis in Athens. It takes its name from this title. (There is a report though that she had a son.)

More than one virgin birth scenario existing for Athena. (1) Zeus produced her by pushing her out through his forehead. (2) Zeus' head was split open with a two-headed axe and out came Athena, newly born but already clothed and armed with one or more weapons.

ATTIS of Phrygia - Attis is a Mesopotamian (Phrygian) god. His mother, the goddess Ishtar, gave birth to him after swallowing a pomegranate seed or almond. Later, when the Roman and Greeks absorbed him into their religions, Attis' mother became Aphrodite (called Venus by the Romans.) Aphrodite gave birth to Attis through her side.

AUGE - Auge's mother was a mortal woman and his father was a God.

AUGUSTUS - The great Roman Emperor Caesar Augustus' father was purported to be the god Apollo who impregnated his mother while in the form of a snake.

BACCHUS – (1) Semele, mother of the Egyptian Bacchus, was a virgin even after his birth. (2) Also see DIONYSUS.

BEDDOU (Fot) - Beddou was a god of the orient. He was born into royalty in 1027 BC. His mother is said to have remained a virgin. The ruling king sought to kill him at birth as he felt the newborn infant posed a future threat to his throne. Beddou was saved by shepherds and lived in the desert until he was 30. After that he did a great deal of religious teaching.

BUDDIAH (Siddhartha Gautama) - He along with Horus, Mithra, Dionysus and Osiris have the most glaring similarities to Jesus' life as we know it. Buddha was born to the Virgin Maya on December 25th. His birth was announced by a star in the sky and his birth drew wise men presenting costly gifts. He was baptized in water. Buddha healed the sick and fed 500 from a small basket of cakes and even walked on water. He died (on a cross, in some traditions,) was buried but arose again after his tomb was opened by supernatural powers. He ascended into heaven but is expected to return in later days to judge the dead and certain others.

CODOM - In Siam (now Thailand), a wandering sunbeam "caresses" a young lady, and the great deliverer, Codom, was born.

CORYBAS - ?

DANAE: (1) Zeus (called Jupiter by the Roman priests) is said to have turned himself into a "shower of gold" to impregnate Danae. (2) Another way it's put is that Zeus impregnated Danae by "visiting" her as a ray of sunlight (other descriptions also include he visited her as a dove.)

DEMETER - ?

DIONYSUS (Greece) - He along with Horus, Mithra, Buddha, Krishna and Osiris have the most glaring similarities to Jesus' life as we know it. Born of a Virgin on December 25th or January 6th. (December 25th would be the date the ancient Greeks would settle on.) He was placed in a manger. (Mangers were a lot more of a commonplace in those days and where many poor travelers were allowed to stay.) He was a traveling teacher who performed many miracles. He turned water into wine. His followers could eat a sacred meal. He rose from the dead on March 25th. He was called the "Redeemer," "Sin bearer," "King of Kings," "the Anointed One," "Only Begotten Son," "Savior."

(1) One version has DIONYSUS originally impregnated into the human woman Semele but he was taken from Semele's womb and completed his embryonic life in Zeus's thigh.

(2) In another version he is the son of Zeus and the virgin goddess Persephone.

EPAPHUS *(Ephapsis)* - (1) Zeus turned himself into a cloud and had sex with IO (from which she became pregnant.) (2) Io was touched by Zeus's hand and became pregnant.

ESCHYLUS - ?

FOHI (Fuxi) - A nymph bathing in a river in China was "touched" by a lotus plant and the great, divine Chinese sun god Fohi is born. Some claim Fohi has a connection to Noah and his Ark.

FRIGGA - Scandinavian (Norse) goddess Frigg (Frigga) was impregnated by the god Odin and bore a son Balder. Blader would be known as the healer and savior of mankind.

GENGHIS KHAN – Followers of the great Mongol leader claimed his mother even admitted to giving birth virginally to her great son.

GLYCON – A likely fictional son of the God Apollo who supposedly had a miraculous birth.

HAINUWELE (Indonesia) - A man called *Ameta* accidently cut his finger while collecting sap from a coconut tree and a baby girl, Hainuwele ("coconut branch"), emerges from the mixture of blood and sap.

HELEN OF TROY – (Also known as Helen of Sparta) - Helen was born thanks to the mating of Zeus and Leda or Nemesis. Zeus took the form of a swan for the impregnation. (Eww!)

HEPHAESTUS – Several classical myths assert that Hera (Zeus' wife) was so annoyed at Zeus for having produced a child with someone else (Athena) that she conceived and bore Hephaestus by herself.

HERCULES – (1) Prudence, the virgin mother of the mighty God Hercules said she "knew only Jove" [Jupiter]. (2) Alcmene in 1280 BC said she was a virgin and claimed Zeus as the father of the Greek hero Hercules. (Zeus had disguised himself as her husband and impregnated her.)

HERA – Hera was the wife of Zeus. She gave virgin birth to Typhon (a monster who fought the gods.) She also gave virgin birth to the more respectable Hephaestus.

HERMES - ?

HERTHA - Teutonic virgin goddess Hertha had a son after she was made pregnant by the "heavenly Spirit".

HESUS - Mayence was the virgin-mother of Hesus of the Druids. In pagan traditions that predate Christianity, she is being bathed in light, with a crown of twelve stars on her head and with her foot on the head of a serpent. *This is identical to what's seen in the Book of Revelation.*

HOMER - In his "Hymn to Asclepius", Homer states that his father is the god Apollo and his mother is the daughter of a renowned soldier, King Phlegyas.

HORUS – (Egypt) - He along with Osiris, Mithra, Krishna, Dionysus and Buddha have the most glaring similarities to Jesus' life as we know it. Isis had "spiritual" relations with her deceased husband Osiris and from that became pregnant with Horus. Horus is said to be born on December 25, sometime before 2500 BC. The Egyptian god Thoth helped Isis, the wife of Osiris, to extract from the dismembered Osiris, the semen with which Isis was impregnated to bear Horus.

HUITZILOPOCHTLI OF THE TOLTEC - A woman named Coatlicue, who was cleaning a temple on the Cerro de Coatepec, near Tula, watched a lovely ball of feathers drop from the sky. She took it and stored it in her bosom but couldn't find it after she finished her work. It had gone into her and made her pregnant.

INDRA – (Tibet) - Indra was born from a virgin. Indra was the ruler of the gods of the Veda. He went to heaven after leaving our world.

ION - Created by a mating of Apollo (the Greek god) and the mortal Creusa.

ISAAC - Sarai (Isaac's mother) was "barren" but gave birth to the biblical character Isaac in what was considered by many to be a virgin birth or miraculous impregnation. Here though is a situation where intercourse with a male is thought to have happened but the woman was previously confirmed to be unable to reproduce, so a "miraculous" or virginal impregnation is thought to have occurred here.

ISIS – (Egypt) – (Lived in roughly 2500 BC) - Isis and her son Horus is a virginal birth scenario that scholars think may have been used as the model for Jesus' virgin birth tradition. There also are a surprisingly large number of other activities and experiences that coincidentally both Jesus and Horus' shared. Horus and Jesus both celebrated their birthdays on December 25th, both were crucified, Horus was given the title KRST which means "anointed one", Horus was also resurrected after three days, Horus resurrected Osiris (Jesus resurrected Lazarus), Horus was crucified next to two thieves, Horus also performed many miracles like healing the sick and walking on water, Seth tried to kill Horus (Herod tried to kill Jesus).

JESUS CHRIST - Isaiah 7:14, Matthew 1:18-25, Luke 1:26-38 and Galatians 4:4 write that Jesus was born of a virgin. Here is part of the Scriptural account of Jesus' virginal conception:

"In the sixth month the angel Gabriel was sent from God to a city of Galilee named Nazareth, to a virgin betrothed to a man whose name was Joseph, of the house of David; and the virgin's name was Mary. And he came to her and said, "Hail, full of grace, the Lord is with you!" But she was greatly troubled at the saying, and considered in her mind what sort of greeting this might be.

"And the angel said to her, "Do not be afraid, Mary, for you have found favor with God. And behold, you will conceive in your womb and bear a son, and you shall call his name Jesus. He will be great, and will be called the Son of the Most High; and the Lord God will give to him the throne of his father David, and he will reign over the house of Jacob for ever; and of his kingdom there will be no end."

"And Mary said to the angel, "How shall this be, since I know not man?" And the angel said to her, "The Holy Spirit will come upon you, and the power of the Most High will overshadow you; therefore the child to be born will be called holy, the Son of God. And behold, your kinswoman Elizabeth in her old age has also conceived a son; and this is the sixth month with her who was called barren. For with God nothing will be impossible."

"And Mary said, "Behold, I am the handmaid of the Lord; let it be to me according to your word." And the angel departed from her" (Luke 1:26-38).

Actually, Jesus being born to a virgin may also have to do with Roman politics. Caesar Augustus, the great Roman Emperor, was said to be of virgin birth. This was used as an argument for why he (Augustus) should be obeyed. In fact there are many records in which he is referred to as *Augustus Son of God*. Because of all this, various historians believe that the Jesus' virgin birth account was also a criticism of the Roman empire.

One other thing to consider is that Jesus was named *Yeshua eban Marian*, (Jesus son of Mary.) It's quite possible that the virgin birth account was mainly to explain why he was not *Jesus son of Joseph* (which is usually how a man back then was identified.) This way his unwed mother was less likely to be accused of sexual wrongdoing.

JOHN THE BAPTIST - The Gospel of Luke makes reference to John the Baptist's infancy. He's described as the son of Zachariah, (who's an old man,) and his wife Elizabeth, who was sterile. Here though is a situation where intercourse happened but the woman was previously confirmed or thought to be unable to reproduce, thus a "miraculous" birth (pregnancy) occurred here.

JULIUS CAESAR - Julius Caesar was purportedly of virgin birth. It was said that he was the son of Cronis Celestine and fathered by the coolest of all Roman gods, Jupiter.

KABIR - The scared Hindu Kabir was said to have been born of a virgin widow (a Hindu), through the palm of her hand. This story of Kabir's birth intended to legitimize Kabir's religious authority in the eyes of the Hindu population who revered his works. Confirmation of this however is absent in Muslim and Sikh accounts of Kabir's work.

KARNA – Karna, (aka Radheya) is one of the central characters in the ancient Indian (India) epic Mahābhārata. The birth of Karna was the result of Queen Kunti asking the god Surya for a child without taking Kunti's virginity, as she was about to marry King Pandu and was expected to still be a virgin.

KAGUYA-HIME (Japan) – (Also known as Princess Kaguya) - The Tale of the Bamboo Cutter (Taketori Monogatari) is a 10th century Japanese folktale. It's likely the oldest extant Japanese narrative. It primarily describes the life and times of a mysterious girl named Kaguya-hime who was discovered as a baby inside the stalk of a glowing bamboo plant.

KINTARŌ (Japan) – (Often translated as "Golden Boy".) ?

KORE – ?

KRISHNA (Chrishna) - The mother of Chrishna (Devaki) was "overshadowed" (taken sexually) by the supreme god, Brahma. Chrishna's mother had given birth seven times before but still remained a virgin (as was the case with Mary who gave birth to 3 boys, including Jesus, and also still remained a virgin.) Krishna's birth was announced by a star. Krishna was born in a cave, which at the time of his birth was miraculously illuminated. King Kansa sought the life of the Indian Christ by ordering the massacre of all male children born during the same night at Chrishna. Krishna traveled widely, performing miracles including raising the dead, healing lepers, the blind and the deaf. The crucified Krishna is pictured on the cross with arms extended. Pierced by an arrow while hanging on the cross, Krishna died, but descended into Hell from which He rose again on the third day and ascended into Heaven. (The Gospel of Nicodemus tell of Jesus' descent into Hell.) He is expected to return on the last day. Chrishna birthday is often thought to be December 25th. (Others claim that Krishna's birth was in July, August or September.)

LEDA - ?

MARJATTA – (In Finnish and Karelian mythology) - While herding, Marjatta ate a lingonberry and becomes pregnant from it. She gave birth to a boy who grew up to be the king of Karelia.

MARDUK – Marduk was the central god in the Babylonian empire. He was patron of the city, which today is located in Iraq. Marduk was also the god of air, earth, and fertility. The Akkadian "Creation Epic" describes his birth that is thought to be much like Jesus'.

MARS – Mars is the very important Roman god of war. The Romans believed that his mother, the Roman goddess Juno, conceived him after being impregnated (or touched) by a flower.

MARY - Mother Mary's birth is seen in various Christian traditions, (particularly Catholic, Orthodox and Anglican) as miraculous. Tradition has it that the Virgin Mary's parents, St. Joachim and St. Anne were childless when an angel came to them and informed them that they would give birth to a daughter (Mary). Mary's mother was thus preserved from the stain of original sin.

MELANIPPE - ?

MILETUS - ?

MINOS – One account has him born of a specially selected mortal woman and a god

MITHRA - "Christianity's sister religion." He along with Horus, Osiris, Krishna, Dionysus and Buddha have the most glaring similarities to Jesus' life as we know it. Mithra had a virgin birth of a sort, Mithra was said to be born from the "rock of a cave" while shepherds and many Magi looked on.
   Mithra came to be known as the all important sun God. He originally was a Zoroastrian God which people began to associate independently of Zoroastrianism. *Mithraism is often called Christianity's "sister religion" largely because there are so many similarities between the two and it originated and was popular prior to Christianity.* Mithraism spread into Greek and Roman influenced areas from Persia, coming to Rome in 68 B.C. It, and the worship of Greek and Roman Gods, were Christianity's biggest competition until the later 3rd century. In fact, until the later 3rd century, it was a more popular religion than Christianity.

Many of Mithraism's doctrines are strikingly similar to Christianity. In particular, communion, the use of holy water, the adoration of shepherds at Mithras' birth, the use of Sundays for the Sabbath instead of the traditional Saturday which is the Sabbath of the Jewish people and using the date of December 25th as the birth date of both Jesus and Mithra, (it had been celebrated as Mithra's birth date for many years before Christians adopted it for Jesus.) Also the Mithraic belief in the immortality of the soul, the last judgment and the resurrection preceded Christianity's adopting those beliefs. However, it's different from Christianity in significant ways also. Mithra was considered a God not a prophet. Its secretive ceremonies excluded women. They also had other lesser gods.

Mithraism was quite popular with Roman soldiers. Though it preached brotherly love, as with Islam and Sikhism, it wished to aid the soldier in battle. People becoming Mithraistic were often baptized in the blood of a bull. After Christianity became Rome's official religion, Christians destroyed most of the Mithratic temples and killed any Mithratic clergy they could find.

Mithraism exposed millions of people to doctrines and procedures which would later be preached by the newcomer, Christianity. Its similarities with Christianity may have made it easier for Christian doctrines to have been so quickly and readily accepted. Had Christianity not been so successful, it's possible Mithraism would have become the official religion of Rome.

MOMOTARŌ (Japan) – (aka The Peach Boy) - Momotarō came to earth inside a giant peach which was found floating down a river by a childless, old woman who was washing clothes at the river.

ODYSSEUS – (Central character in Homer's epic "The Odyssey") - Though it's disputed, he's thought to have had a virgin birth. He was also a carpenter and had other similarities to Jesus.

ORISHAS or emissaries of God - ORISHA AJE (one of the Orishas) was said to have come to the world for the sole purpose of redeeming humanity from sin. He was called *Orisha Imole* (deity of light), *The Redeemer, etc*. He was crucified and later ascended to the heavens.

OSIRIS (EGYPT) – He along with Horus, Krishna, Mithra, Dionysus and Buddha have the most glaring similarities to Jesus' life as we know it. (Osiris is thought to have been born within the last five days of the Egyptian calendar year. While the 25th is the most popular day for his birthday, technically there are 4 other days he could have been born on.)

PAN - His father is often thought to be the Greek god Hermes who mated with a shepherdess or nymph to give birth to Pan.

PANDAVAS (the) - In Hinduism, Brahmin laid a curse upon King Pandu. Brahmin told King Pandu that if he touched either of his two wives sexually the king would die. Queen Kunti (one of his wives) asked the other gods to give her and her co-wife children without having to copulate with the king. The gods gave them the Pandavas.

PERICTIONE – The Greek god Apollo appeared to Ariston in a dream and impregnated her with Perictione.

PERSEUS – (1) His mother (Danae) conceived him with Jupiter (Zeus) who impregnated her in the form of a golden shower (2) Zeus came to Danae as a shower of gold flakes.

PERSEPHONE – She was known as the virgin maiden. One account has her giving birth to Dionysus after having been impregnated by Zeus who likely used a lightning bolt to impregnate her.

PLATO – A story has spread and stuck. It asserts that Plato was the son of the Greek god Apollo (not Ariston, Plato's father) and Amphictione. Ariston supposedly had a vision in his sleep which forbade him to have intercourse with his wife for ten months. During that time she mysteriously became pregnant presumably thanks to Apollo.

PROMETHEUS - Prometheus descended from heaven to save mankind.

PYTHAGORAS – Pythagoras was said to have been conceived by a specter or ghost of the God Apollo. Pythais was his mother.

QI - *The Abandoned One*, later known as *Houji* – A Chinese culture hero or god of agriculture. Records report him to have been miraculously conceived when his mother, the consort Jiang Yuan, stepped into a footprint left by the supreme god Shangdi.

QUETZALCOATL - Quetzalcoatl was born of a virgin around 900 BC. His story is told by the Aztecs and Mayans. He was crucified. He was considered the God of light that struggled against the god of darkness called Tezcatlipoca. He was associated with the planet Venus, the morning star, like Jesus is. The cross was used as a symbolic representation. He said he would return from the dead to claim his earthly kingdom.

QUEXALCOTE – We are told that *Chimalman*, mother of Quexalcote, was a still a virgin after his birth. It's also stated that he also had a crucifixion and a resurrection after three days.

QUIRRNUS - Quirrnus was born of a virgin.

RA (RE): The Egyptian sun god of Kimit (Sais or Egypt). He made himself pregnant (asexually) then gave birth to air and moisture.

RHEA - ?

REMUS – Remus' mother is stated to be Rhea Silvia and his father the god Mars. Rhea was "ravished" in a garden by Mars.

ROMULUS – Romulus' mother is stated to be Rhea Silvia and his father the god Mars. Rhea was "ravished" in a garden by Mars.

SAKIA - Maia was his virgin mother.

SCIPIO AFRICANUS - His mother was a mortal woman and his father was a god.

SUCHIQUECAL – Suchiquecal, the Queen of Heaven, is said to have conceived a son without sex with a man.

TAMERLANE OF BERMUDA - Tamerlane's mother got pregnant with him after having had sex with "the God of Day."

TARCHETIUS' MAIDSERVANT - The King of the Albans, Tarchetius, saw an apparition of a penis rise out of the fireplace and remain there for a number of days. Roman priests told him that a virgin must have sex with the apparition. A maidservant or slave was forced to and had twins.

THESEUS – Plutarch notes that Theseus may have been born with the assistance "the gods" (likely Neptune.) He also states that Theseus' grandfather Pittheus may have invented the story that claims Theseus was the child of Neptune.

THOTH - ?

TIAMAT: One of Babylonian religion's first two gods. *She gave virgin birth to many of the gods of the Mesopotamia.*

TAMMUZ – Tammuz was born before 2600 BC and was hailed as the only begotten son of the god Ea. His mother was a virgin and famous goddess by the name of Ishtar.

TIEN (China) – Tien was born of a virgin.

VIRGIL (Famous Roman poet) - In "The Secret History of Virgil" by Alexander Neckam, Magia Pollia (Virgil's mother) is said to have been impregnated by the god Jupiter (Zeus) who came to her in the form of a shower of gold-leaf flakes which blew in through her window and landed in her wine glass. From that she became pregnant with and gave birth to the great poet Virgil.

VULCAN - Juno conceived Vulcan after being immaculately impregnated by the wind.

XACA OF CHINA – Maia, the mother of the Savior Xaca, was impregnated by a white elephant which she saw in her sleep. Xaca exited her through one of her sides.

YESHUA – See Jesus Christ.

YU (emporer) – YU was founder of the Chinese Xia (Hsia) Dynasty and the first Chinese monarch. (1) Shing-Mon was the virgin mother of this Chinese Bodisatva Yu. A star indicates the birth place of Yu. Like many oriental saviors, Yu is born out of his mother's side. (2) Another version has Emporer Yu conceived when his mother was struck with a star while traveling.

ZAGREUS - Persephone was the virgin mother of the lesser known Greek god Zagreus. It's possible Zagreus is Hades (Pluto) son.

ZOROASTER/ZARATHUSTRA – As of 1990 it only an estimated 250,000 believers, primarily in India and Iran. This religion and it's offshoot religion, Mithraism, has had a tremendous impact on the development of Christianity and Judaism.

Founded by the Persian prophet Zoroaster sometime between 1000 and 600 B.C., it's one of the world's original *dualistic* religions (see glossary for definition of dualism). It was practiced most by people in Arabia, and south-central Asia. Verifiable history shows it flourishing in the Persian empire by 550 B.C.

After Alexander the Great's invasion of Persia (334 B.C.,) Zoroastrianism lost most of its followers. It wouldn't experience a serious revival for hundreds of years. Zoroastrianism once again lost popularity when in roughly 637 A.D., Islamic forces conquered much of the territory it was practiced in, forcibly replacing it with Islam.

Like Christianity, Zoroastrianism is dualistic. It preaches that there is a struggle between good and evil forces for mastery of the universe. The good God and creator of the universe, is Ahura Mazda. The evil demon is Ahriman and he's bent on destroying everything good in the universe.

Zoroaster was sent down by God (Ahura Mazda) to help humans fight evil. He received the sacred laws of God, the Avesta on Mount Sabalan, in Persia. If an individual were to choose the path of goodness which Zoroaster represents, then on Judgment Day, he/she would go to heaven. At some point, a great battle between God, his angels (the "Amesha Spenta") and those "good" converted humans will occur against the evil demons and "bad" people who have not "converted." This will be the final battle and be the final "Judgement of the Dead.*" *Since this was preached, at least in Jesus' area, six to ten centuries before Jesus was even born, it's history's original "Judgment Day."* Peace will reign on earth after this battle because it is now cleansed of evil (unlike the Christian version of Judgement Day which assumes it is the end of the world.)

Many similarities exist between Zoroastrianism, Judaism and Christianity. Both Zoroaster and Moses got their respective religious "Laws" from their one true God on a mountain (he getting the Avesta from Ahura Mazda on Mt. Sabalan and Moses getting the Judaic "laws" from Yahweh on Mt. Sinai.) Each is dualistically fighting a power of evil, Ahura Mazda against Ahriman, and Yahweh and the God of Christianity against Satan. The Zoroastrian all important first period of creation is divided into 6 parts as the Old Testament account of creation is divided into six days. A human couple is the first human beings for each religion, Moshya and Moshyana by the Zoroastrian account and Adam and Eve by the other two religious accounts. A terrible winter was sent by Ahura Mazda, as told in the Avesta, to punish mankind for its evil. This, of course, parallels the great flood theory. All three religions believes in a good life after death for the righteous and a hellish life after death for the unrighteous. A Zoroastrian, during a religious ceremony, drinks milk and water and eats bread. Originally, Christians did the same with wine and unleavened bread (now it's more often wafer.) Zoroastrians celebrated high and low masses. A religion worshipping the lesser Zoroastrian God of light, Mithra, spread from Persia to the Mediterranean and even Rome. In fact, in Rome, it was a more popular religion than Christianity for almost the first three centuries A. D. Various Christian assertions including the date of December 25th for the traditional birthday of Jesus, comes from Mithraism (Mithra's birthday was celebrated on December 25th for many years prior to Jesus' birth.) For more information on what's called *Christianity's sister religion*, see the description of Mithraism in this section.

ZUNIS - Celestine, the mother of Zunis is said to have been a virgin.

Epilogue

It may be interesting to note that the word "virgin" in both Hebrew (almah) and Greek (parthenos) means a mature young woman and not necessarily a woman who has never had intercourse. Where it is written in Isaiah 7:14, "behold a virgin shall conceive and bear a son," (the Old Testament parable which asserts that the coming Messiah will be of virgin birth,) literally it does not specify that the "virgin" mother would in fact never previously had had intercourse. It might be prophesying that a younger woman would be the mother rather than a middle aged woman.

Doctrine of Perpetual Virginity - Roman Catholic doctrine asserting that Mother Mary lived, gave virgin birth to Jesus and remained a virgin through her entire life.

Gods, Deities and Prophets Who's Birthday Traditionally is Thought to be on December 25 (though in some cases not all followers agree).

(The below were also presented and better described in the previous list.)

ATTIS
BEDDOU
BUDDIAH
DIONYSUS
KRISHNA
HERCULES
HORUS
MITHRA
QUETZALCOATL
TAMMUZ

Major World Religions

ANIMISM - It's thought to be the world's first and oldest religion. Followers believe every single thing, object and phenomena has a "spirit" and importance, thus it must be respected. It's still the religion of countless millions.

BUDDHISM - Founded around 2,500 years ago by a prince named Siddhartha, Buddhism was originally an Indian religion. The prince received the Sanskrit (an Indian language) title of Buddha. Its translation is "the enlightened one." As was the case when Jesus was born, prophecy in Buddha's area was that a great spiritual leader was about to emerge. After a revelation, Buddha gave up all his possessions and searched for the meaning of life. It's said that after sitting under a tree for 49 days, he achieved Nirvana (enlightenment.) Buddha felt suffering was due to desire. By eliminating desire, passion and ego, one has the best chance for attaining enlightenment.

Many sacred Buddhist books are in a collection called the Pali Canon. There are at least 256 million Buddhists (1980 estimate.)

CHRISTIANITY - Based primarily on the sacred classical Christian books and letters compiled in the Bible. The Bible is comprised of (1) selected reports and interpretations of the founding prophet, Jesus Christ (New Testament) and (2) the old Hebrew sacred books (Old Testament.) Jesus was born Hebrew and spent his life as a Hebrew. Thus his name at birth was also Hebrew. That name was "Yehoshua." Another rendering of Yehoshua is Joshua. "Jesus" is the Greek translation of the Hebrew name, Joshua (meaning savior.) *Ho Christos* is Greek for "an anointed one." Over the years, Ho Christos was shortened to just "Christ." It's doubtful anyone ever addressed Jesus during his lifetime as "Jesus Christ" as his following was overwhelmingly Hebrew not Greek. Also the Greek speaking folks in his area wouldn't have any problems calling people by their Hebrew names. "Bible" is the English translation of the Latin word for books "Biblia."

Though we presently call the Bible "Bible," if we were living roughly four centuries and prior to that, we would call it "Biblia," not "Bible" because English was not a popular language like today. As Latin was the language of the church, this collection of books was for over a millennium referred to by the masses by it's Latin name "Biblia."

There are approximately 1.8 billion Christians worldwide. (Early to mid 1990s estimate.) That includes 806 million Catholics, 74 million Eastern Orthodox Christians (Eastern Europe, Asia and Africa) and 343 million Protestants. The latter two branches don't consider the pope to be their leader.

Central to traditional Christian theology are the "Four Spiritual Laws." (1) God allowed his only son, Jesus Christ, to die for our sins and Adam & Eve's "Original Sin." (2) Man is sinful and bad from birth and needs help knowing the goodness that is God. (3) The only way for man to go to heaven and know God is through Jesus Christ. This cannot be done through any other religion and depending on which branch of Christianity one belongs to, it cannot be done through any other branch.) (4) Each individual has to open up his or her "heart" and receive Jesus. Everybody who doesn't do this, and those who belong to any other religion or perhaps Christian branch, will automatically go to hell.

CONFUCIANISM - Developed 2,500 years ago by the Chinese philosopher K'ung Fu-tzu, who was formally known as "The Master Kung." It's technically not a religion, though it's often treated like one. Confucius himself never claimed divinity.

Confucianism is more oriented toward specifying principles of good social conduct, practical wisdom, and proper social relationships. Its had a tremendous influence on the sociological development of China. A very "evolved" Confucian would be a "Chun-tzu," a "perfect gentleman."

Throughout the years, it's been interwoven with other conquering religions but still survives today with around 175 million followers (1980 estimate.)

HINDUISM - Found primarily in India, it advocates the same anti-materialistic outlook as Buddhism and Jainism. The word "Hindu" comes from the Sanskrit word Sindhu, meaning river. Around 1500 B.C., Persians immigrants migrating west through Pakistan called Pakistan's giant river valley "Hind." Over time, the people living in what is now India, became known as Hindus. Their religion took on their name.

There are many gods worshipped by various followers. The main gods are Brahma, Vishnu and Shiva. Brahma is the creator of the world. Shiva is a God who represents the eternal cycle of creation and destruction. Vishnu is a protector, a caring God who watches over people who worship him. The most popular scared Hindu text is the Bhagavad Gita, meaning "Song of the Lord." It is a holy poem made up of around 700 verses written between 200 B.C. and 200 A.D.

Hinduism has roughly 500 million followers (1980s figure.)

ISLAM - Mohammed, the founding prophet of Islam, was born in Mecca and lived from 570-632 A.D. "Islam" means submission. Followers are known as Muslims or Moslems which is Arabic for "those who submit." Islam has more than a billion converts and is the fastest growing religion in the world.

At age forty, the Archangel Gabriel (the same angel who came to Mary, mother of Jesus and told her that her son was to be very special,) is said to have come to Mohammed in a
vision. Gabriel is said to have told him that he was a prophet and should spread the teachings of only one God, Allah.

Mohammed preached a holy war, a "Jihad" against nonbelievers. During his lifetime, conquests, as well as treaties with surrounding areas, gave him and his religion control of Arabia. Presently though, the majority of Islam's followers aren't from Arabia.

Muslims believe *"There is no God but Allah, and Mohammed is his messenger."* Biblical Christian and Judaic prophets, including Jesus, are respected but only considered to have come to earth to prepare the masses for the most important prophet, Mohammed.

Islam also believes in a "Day of Judgment" when the good will go to paradise and the bad will go to hell. The Islamic holiest of books is the Koran. Muslim soldiers are generally assured a place in heaven if they die fighting for Allah.

JAINISM - Followers of the various sects of Jainism are primarily located in northern India. They broke off from traditional Hinduism in the 6th century B.C. Its founder was Vardhamana Jnatiputra Mahavira.

Followers abhor killing any form of life and that includes insects. They're not allowed to be butchers and soldiers. Their diet may not include meat or fish.

Mahatma Gandhi, though Hindu, was brought up in a very Jainist influenced area. His doctrine of nonviolence may have developed from this Jainist influence.

There are roughly 200 million followers of Jainism, though many are also Hindu.

JUDAISM - While its earliest origins were polytheistic (having more than one God,) it evolved into the oldest, consistently monotheistic (one God) religion.

(Around 1400 B.C., the Egyptian pharaoh Amenhotep IV temporarily converted the Egyptian religion to monotheism by ordering everybody to worship a single almighty God, Aton. This made them the first people in recorded history to be monotheistic. However, the Egyptians eagerly reverted to polytheism shortly after the pharaoh's death.)

Judaism's monotheistic origins are said to be when Jehovah, also called Yahweh, (the Jewish names for God,) spoke to Abraham and promised him the land of Canaan (Israel) for his descendants, assuming they spread the doctrine that there was only one God. In 66 A.D., the Jewish people rose up against the Roman oppressors but were crushed four years later. *40% of all Jews in the world were said to have been killed. Almost all Jews the Romans captured were sold into slavery.* The Jews would not have their promised land again *for almost 1900 years.* They have it now and it's called Israel. The most important Hebrew writings are in their sacred "Torah." There are roughly 18 million Jewish people world-wide and millions more who are casual followers.

MITHRAISM - Mithra came to be known as the all important sun God. He originally was a Zoroastrian God which people began to associate independently of Zoroastrianism. *Mithraism is often called Christianity's "sister religion" largely because there are so many similarities between the two and it originated and was popular prior to Christianity.* Mithraism spread into Greek and Roman influenced areas from Persia, coming to Rome in 68 B.C. It, and the worship of Greek and Roman Gods, were Christianity's biggest competition until the later 3rd century. In fact, until the later 3rd century, it was a more popular religion than Christianity.

Many of Mithraism's doctrines are strikingly similar to Christianity. In particular, communion, the use of holy water, the adoration of shepherds at Mithras' birth, the use of Sundays for the Sabbath instead of the traditional

Saturday which is the Sabbath of the Jewish people and using the date of December 25th as the birth date of both Jesus and Mithra, (it had been celebrated as Mithra's birth date for many years before Christians adopted it for Jesus.) Also the Mithraic belief in the immortality of the soul, the last judgment and the resurrection preceded Christianity's adopting those beliefs. However, it's different from Christianity in significant ways also. Mithra was considered a God not a prophet. Its secretive ceremonies excluded women. They also had other lesser gods.

Mithraism was quite popular with Roman soldiers. Though it preached brotherly love, as with Islam and Sikhism, it wished to aid the soldier in battle. People becoming Mithraistic were often baptized in the blood of a bull. After Christianity became Rome's official religion, Christians destroyed most of the Mithratic temples and killed any Mithratic clergy they could find.

Mithraism exposed millions of people to doctrines and procedures which would later be preached by the newcomer, Christianity. Its similarities with Christianity may have made it easier for Christian doctrines to have been so quickly and readily accepted. Had Christianity not been so successful, it's possible Mithraism would have become the official religion of Rome.

MAOISM - At one time it had an estimated 800 million followers.

While many don't consider it a religion, the Chinese government considers it to at least be something like it.

Maoism means "Mao Tse-tung's Thought." The "Bible" of Maoism is a book called "Quotations from the Works of Chairman Mao Tse-tung." As of 1975, it was the second largest selling book in the world after the Bible. As with the Bible, it is used for inspiration and solving emotional and historical dilemmas.

The main principles of Maoism are said to be faith in the Communist Party, faith in the masses, and putting the needs of the masses ahead of your own personal desires. Maoism doesn't have as much clout as it did a generation ago but it remains a very important influence in China.

SCIENTISM -The belief that science can better answer questions formerly designated for theology, has inspired it to be classified by millions as a religion.

The study of science is said to officially begin with the Greek intellectuals. For many centuries, scientists worked in secret as they could be confused with madmen or heretics.

Scientism is the belief that the primary and/or best way to understand the universe is determined by scientifically acquired knowledge. Like other religions, followers tend to believe that their's is the only true "religion." In their opinion, other religions, while not necessarily bad, are largely built on unproven theories.

By far the focus of Scientism is research in its 1,200 plus fields (Botany, Physics, Chemistry etc.)

SHINTOISM -The original, and currently the primary religion of Japan. It's been significantly influenced by Buddhism and Confucianism. The word Shinto comes from the Chinese words "Shin Tao," meaning "the way of the gods."

Originally, followers worshipped a number of gods but this began to change as Buddhism became more popular in Japan.

Shintoism was revived in the 18th century and became, by government decree, the country's official religion in 1867. The Japanese emperor, according to the Shintoism of the day, was descended from the sun goddess Amaterasu Omikami. Having emperors who were descended from gods, unlike any other country's leaders, made many Japanese feel they were the world's most superior people and thus destined to rule the earth. This philosophy provoked their great military build-up and their insatiable appetite for conquests. After their World War II surrender, General MacArthur and the emperor revoked Shintoism as the state religion. It was also changed so it does not officially assert the emperor's "divinity."

There are approximately 3.4 million followers of Shintoism (though millions more who are casual followers.)

SIKHISM - Founded around 1500 A.D. in an area of northwest India called Punjab.

Its founder, Nanak, was the first of their ten gurus. Their main scriptures are in the "Adi Granth" which is Punjabi (a language) for "The Original Book." This was compiled in 1604. Sikhism's original aim was to combine the Hindu and Mohammedan (Islamic) religions into one. Sikhs believe in exercising allegiance to one God, morality in their endeavors and military proficiency. They established a sizable empire but lost it to the British in the Sikh wars. There are roughly 14 million believers worldwide.

TAOISM - Considered by Chinese tradition to be founded by Li Erh in the 6th century B.C. Along the way, his name was changed to Lao-tze meaning "Old Master." The main text of Taoism is in the book Tao-te-Ching which tradition asserts Lao-tze wrote. It's perhaps best known in the west for the concept of Yin and Yang.

Taoism teaches that tranquility and happiness can be found in humility, optimism, being passive and developing inner peace.

This philosophy/religion is highly regarded by many people in China but is banned by the communist government.

Due largely to religious persecution, its followers have dwindled to an estimated 30 to 60 million.

ZOROASTRIANISM - While it currently has only an estimated 250,000 believers (1990), primarily in India and Iran, this religion and it's offshoot religion, Mithraism, has had a tremendous impact on the development of Christianity and Judaism.

Founded by the Persian prophet Zoroaster sometime between 1000 and 600 B.C., it's one of the world's original *dualistic* religions (see glossary for definition of dualism). It was practiced most by people in Arabia, and south-central Asia. Verifiable history shows it flourishing in the Persian empire by 550 B.C.

After Alexander the Great's invasion of Persia (334 B.C.,) Zoroastrianism lost most of its followers. It wouldn't experience a serious revival until hundreds of years later. Zoroastrianism once again lost popularity when in roughly 637 A.D., Islamic forces conquered much of the territory it was practiced in, forcibly replacing it with Islam.

Like Christianity, Zoroastrianism is dualistic. It preaches that there is a struggle between good and evil forces for mastery of the universe. The good God and creator of the universe, is Ahura Mazda. The evil demon is Ahriman and he's bent on destroying everything good in the universe.

Zoroaster was sent down by God (Ahura Mazda) to help humans fight evil. He received the sacred laws of God, the Avesta on Mount Sabalan, in Persia. If an individual were to choose the path of goodness which Zoroaster represents, then on Judgment Day, he/she would go to heaven. At some point, a great battle between God, his angels (the "Amesha Spenta") and those "good" converted humans will occur against the evil demons and "bad" people who have not "converted." This will be the final battle and be the final "Judgement of the Dead." *Since this was preached, at least in Jesus' area, six to ten centuries before Jesus was even born, it's history's original "Judgment Day."* Peace will reign on earth after this battle because it is now cleansed of evil (unlike the Christian version of Judgement Day which assumes it is the end of the world.)

Many similarities exist between Zoroastrianism, Judaism and Christianity. Both Zoroaster and Moses got their respective religious "Laws" from their one true God on a mountain (he getting the Avesta from Ahura Mazda on Mt. Sabalan and Moses getting the Judaic "laws" from Yahweh on Mt. Sinai.) Each is dualistically fighting a power of evil, Ahura Mazda against Ahriman, and Yahweh and the God of Christianity against Satan. The Zoroastrian all important first period of creation is divided into 6 parts as the Old Testament account of creation is divided into six days. A human couple is the first human beings for each religion, Moshya and Moshyana by the Zoroastrian account and Adam and Eve by the other two religious accounts. A terrible winter was sent by Ahura Mazda, as told in the Avesta, to punish mankind for its evil. This, of course, parallels the great flood theory. All three religions believes in a good life after death for the righteous and a hellish life after death for the unrighteous. A Zoroastrian, during a religious ceremony, drinks milk and water and eats bread. Originally, Christians did the same with wine and unleavened bread (now it's more often wafer.) Zoroastrians celebrated high and low masses. A religion worshipping the lesser Zoroastrian God of light, Mithra, spread from Persia to the Mediterranean and even Rome. In fact, in Rome, it was a more popular religion than Christianity for almost the first three centuries A. D. Various Christian assertions including the date of December 25th for the traditional birthday of Jesus, comes from Mithraism (Mithra's birthday was celebrated on December 25th for many years prior to Jesus' birth.) For more information on what's called *Christianity's sister religion*, see the description of Mithraism in this section.

GLOSSARY

AHIMSA: The belief, primarily by Buddhists, Jainists and Hindus, that killing another living thing, no matter how seemingly insignificant (for example a termite,) is unacceptable. In their opinion, all living things have fairly similar souls. These souls dwell in various physical life forms in a complex cycle of reincarnation. It's possible that a human could eat all or part of a plant, animal, etc., which housed the soul of an ancestor. This could screw up the cycle of reincarnation and cause great concern.

ANTINOMIANISM: States that society's laws do not apply to Christians because they are governed, unlike any other religion, by the divine grace of God.

ANTHROPOMORPHISM: The assumption that God has the same or many of the same types of emotional characteristics as humans.

ARIANS: A largely Gnostic and extremely popular "heretical" branch of Christianity founded by the Greek theologian Arius in roughly 318 A.D. They claimed God is not understandable and not involved with life on earth. Christ was worshipped as a major prophet but considered human instead of the son of God. Two major branches of Christianity had developed by the early 4th century, the Arians, and a branch headed by another Greek theologian, Athanasius which would eventually become the Catholics. The historic Council of Nicaea was called in 325 A.D. by Roman emperor Constantine I (who declared tolerance for Christianity 13 years earlier.) There they decided which of the two "types" of Christianity would become the "official Christianity." The Arians lost and 200,000 were killed as heretics over a several century period. [1]

ATHEISM: The religious conviction that God does not exist.

CATHARS OF LANBUEDOC:

Languedoc is considered one of the most beautiful sections of France. In the later 1100's, it had developed into a thriving, cultured province complete with an active seaport. Its largest city was Toulouse. Some of France's most renowned early poets came from this area and were living during this time. Jews were treated better here than in most of Europe.

At that time, Languedoc was the cultural and commercial center of southwestern Europe, but it had a very serious problem. It was the headquarters for a religion that the Catholic Church had forbidden, Catharism.

The Cathars evolved from the ancient Gnostics. Like Christianity, the Cathars believed in the duality of good and evil. However, over the centuries they developed several major principles which conflicted with the Catholic Church. To them, God had two sons. The oldest son, Lucifer, upset God (his father) and got himself kicked out of heaven. Lucifer was the one who made man and planned on holding man in bondage until God let Lucifer back up into heaven. They expected the end of the world at anytime. Like the early Christians, whom they considered to be their role models, they subscribed to a life of poverty and abstinence. They considered material worth evil and many were quite poor. Even Saint Bernard, who disapproved of them, wrote *"As for the morals of the heretic, he cheats no one, he opposes no one, he strikes no one; his cheeks are pale with fasting,...his hands labor for his livelihood."* [3]

The Cathars considered themselves Christians, but rejected the Catholic Church as the source of all Christian authority. They rejected the cross as a symbol and rejected the sacraments. Unlike the Catholic Church, the Cathar priest had no church in which to preach since that is a material thing. Instead he went from town to town in black robes, preaching, praying, working the fields and tending to the sick.

Pope Innocent III was elected in 1198 and he had ambitious plans for the papacy. "To Peter [a synonym for the Pope*] was left the governance not only of the universal church [Catholicism] but of the whole world."* [4] First he sent the Teutonic knights northward along the Baltic on Crusades to "help" the Letts and Livonians of northeastern Europe be saved (yes there were many Christian crusades that weren't in the holy land.) He also decided it was time to deal with the "heretical" folks in Languedoc.

In 1207, the pope formally demanded that the leaders of Languedoc eliminate these "heretics" from their territories and convert it to a bastion of Roman Catholic theology. The area had enjoyed comparative religious tolerance as part of their very developed culture. Carrying out this demand would be difficult. The lord of the area, Count Raymond VI, politely declined the order. He was then excommunicated. The church took away title of all his lands including the heart of Languedoc, the town of Toulouse (this is something the church often did back then since according to them, God owned everything and they represented God.)

Seeing that fighting the most powerful leader in Europe, the pope, was a losing cause, Raymond VI suddenly changed his mind and joined the anti-Cathar bandwagon. He had to surrender seven castles as part of his atonement and release from excommunication, which he did. Meanwhile Pope Innocent III had called for a Crusade to eliminate the Languedoc "heretics." The church was willing to make a very enticing offer to those who joined. For 40 days of military service, they would receive forgiveness for all their sins and safety from their creditors. Soon 20,000 knights and 200,000 peasants had begun what would be called the Albigensian Crusade.

The first city the army attacked was Bezier, burning it to the ground and killing 15,000. [5] During this wasting of Bezier, the Catholic leader was asked by the Crusaders, "Lord, what shall we do? We cannot distinguish the good from the wicked?" The abbot reportedly said the now famous *"kill them all! God will recognize his own"'*. The Papal envoy wrote the pope that the crusaders had killed 15,000 people "showing mercy neither to order nor age nor sex." [6]

The crusade was successful. Most of the opposing fortifications surrendered without a fight. Count Raymond, however, tried to get his lands back. In February of 1211, he was presented with the terms by which the church would allow him back a certain portion of Languedoc. The demands included that he give the clergy all the property they at anytime wanted and banish and cease to protect the Cathars and Jews.

(Remember the Jews have been heavily prejudiced against by the church for being the "Christ-killers." In fact Jews were banished from many kingdoms. The first Jew to go to the new world was with Columbus as Spain had banished all Jews from within their borders that year.)

The Count refused, was excommunicated again and the Crusade continued with a different army. After one battle, four hundred Cathars were burned and 80 sympathizing knights were hung. The leader of the city; a woman by the name of Dame Giraude, was thrown in a pit and buried alive with stones.

Many noblemen, including a Spanish king, would get involved before it was over. Still more crusades would be sent against Languedoc. All 5,000 people in Marmande were slaughtered in 1214. "Men and women, barons, ladies and little children, were all stripped and despoiled and put to the sword," one chronicler wrote. [7]

Before the Albigensian Crusades were over, as many as 500,000 Cathars, Jews, Cathar sympathizers and people unlucky enough to be in the area (including Catholics), had been killed. [8] The Pope's obsession with ridding the planet of this "heretic" had ravaged Languedoc, but it was not over. It was now the 1270's and the inquisitions were about to begin.

CHRISTOLOGY: The study of Jesus (Yehoshua) and his teachings.

CLASSICAL CHRISTIAN: A phrase used to describe persons who at least think they live their lives according to the Bible and other long standing Christian declarations. Synonyms include Christian theist, theist, Christian fundamentalist and anthropomorphist.

CYNICS: An ancient Greek school of philosophy founded around 40 B.C. by a pupil of Socrates, Antisthenes. In its early years, it put great importance on self-control and independence in order to lead a virtuous, righteous life. It evolved and is best remembered for its later doctrines. These asserted that life was a curse and true happiness could come only from enjoying physical desires. They viewed the world and everything in it with contempt, as if the world and humans were not even necessary.

DEISM: The belief that God created the world and the laws of nature. While God acts as the final judge of man, God chooses not to involve itself in mankind's everyday affairs. This allows individuals and society to dictate for themselves, among other things, their own religious course. Deists question the authenticity of prophets, scripture or anything claiming to be directly from God as they deny God's direct involvement in such matters.

DUALISM: A religious doctrine that asserts everything in the universe is subject to the influence of two powerful but opposite forces, one good, one evil. Zoroastrianism, Judaism and Christianity are dualistic religions. God is assumed to be on the side of good and the devil is assumed to be on the side of evil. The Yin and Yang represents Toaism's concept of dualism.

ECCLESIOLOGY: The investigation of what makes up the Christian Church.

EMPIRICISM: The theory that all knowledge is gained from personal experience (or somebody else's.) As all ideas and attitudes are said to develop from experience, it denies that people are born with particular behavior characteristics, something modern psychology disputes.

ESCHATOLOGY: The Christian doctrine of, and study of, Judgment Day, the Second Coming of Christ and the world after the apocalypse.

EXISTENTIALISM: Its origin is attributed to Kierkegaard but it's more often associated with Sartre. It states (1) nobody is predestined to do anything that that individual doesn't consciously and/or subconsciously want to do; (2) every individual must be responsible for his or her own choices and the consequence of their action; (3) all individuals should have and/or strive to have, freedom of choice in as much as possible; (4) individuals should actively seek to learn how to improve their lives and (5) the universe is not considered to be an orderly place and thus it can only be partially understood.

FIDEISM: The theological view that certain religious doctrines cannot be denied or verified by man (such as what God wants, looks like etc.) It asserts the church's view of the subject can be and must be unquestioned, even if the church's knowledge is only based on faith.

FLAGELLANTS: A fanatical, originally anti-Semitic Christian sect formed around 1260. They believed in atoning for their and other's sins by whipping themselves and each other. They often ran through a town's street whipping themselves into a frenzy calling on those watching to repent. People eagerly watched as they whipped each other for hours. The "Black Death" plague years (see "Prayer" chapter) gave them added numbers as God was thought to be very angry. They believed strongly in the apocalypse. In 1349, the pope declared them heretics. In 1369, after their leader and 90 followers were burned to death for heresy, they largely disappeared from Europe until 1820) in Lisbon. Flagellations continue to be part of certain religious ceremonies. A good example is the annual Good Friday whippings in the city of San Fernando in the Philippines.

FREEMASONS: A highly successful fraternal and social organization. Its membership took off after the 14th century. Freemason's doctrines include religious tolerance and equality of all men. Its meetings were often cloaked in secrecy. Church opposition kept them out of predominately Catholic countries.

FREETHINKERS: Originated in the 18th century. One of the first schools of thought to question the divine knowledge of the church. Its religious aim was to make theological conclusions strictly from rules of reason. They rejected as a source of knowledge supernatural authority

(God or gods who speak through people.) A number of freethinkers were imprisoned and executed for heresy.

GNOSTICISM: A combination of a number of "heretical" pagan, Judaic and Christian religious philosophies. The largest Gnostic sects were the Manichaens, Cathars, Arians and the original Christian Gnostics.

Though it may be hard to believe, documentation shows that *many hundreds of thousands of people* in Gnostic sects have been killed as heretics. The largest Gnostic sects were the Manichaens, Cathars, Arians and the other major branch of early Christianity, the original Christian Gnostics.

Gnostic doctrine varied somewhat from sect to sect and century to century but largely it's centered around a battle between good and evil. The world we live in, the "material" world (that which is made of matter) is considered evil and the supernatural "spiritual" world, good. A supremely good God exists but our world, (the material world) was the creation of the devil, the "Demiurge." Followers could expect their souls to travel through several worlds on its way to Gods "divine world of light." As matter (anything made of atoms) is made by the devil, a life of abstinence was the best way to salvation. God sent Jesus Christ as an ambassador of heaven, not as a prophet. Also, the Gnostics didn't consider him the son of God.

HUMANISM: Started in the 14th century and peaked during the renaissance and reformation. Humanism continues to exist today and is represented by several organizations including the American Humanist Association in Amherst, New York. Humanism replaces God with man as the center of worship. The individual's personal growth and happiness are considered "divine." The energy and money that the theist spends on the pursuit of traditional religious endeavors, is considered better spent on making the individual's life on earth more pleasant.

HUSSITES: A Christian sect founded by the Bohemian John Huss (1369?-1415.) He was heavily influenced by the teachings of John Wycliffe, the man who incurred the wrath of the Catholic church by being the first to translate the Bible into English. Hussites preached church reform. The pope sent several European crusades against the Hussites and their supporters. Huss was burned at the stake for heresy.

JANSENISM: Based on principles released posthumously by Cornelius Jansen (1585-1638.) It was bitterly fought by the Jesuits and denounced by numerous popes and governments. Jansenism denied several church doctrines. It was most popular in 17th and 18th century France. When Blaise Pascal entered his religious stage late in life, he became a Jansenist.

JOSEPHUS: (37ish-100ish A.D.) Though contemporary historians view some of his facts with skepticism, two of his surviving works "The Jewish War" and "The Jewish Antiquities" are considered important sources of historical information concerning Jesus' time period and to a certain extent, Jesus (Yehoshua.)

LOGICAL POSITIVISM: Works according to the "verifiability principle." If some thing or theory is unverifiable, then Logical Positivists don't disbelieve it, they just don't take it seriously. The church branded them as atheists since they assert that the study of the supernatural (God) is useless and meaningless as it isn't verifiable scientifically. Philosophy is considered to be a combination of analysis, logic and science. Both Logical Positivism and its philosophical parent, Positivism, are sometimes confused with agnosticism. Agnosticism is more theologically oriented than the Positivism.

MATERIALISM: Considers the universe explainable *only* by the nature of matter. Everything can be explained by the activities of atoms. Analyzing anything without atomic structure is considered useless. That includes the supernatural (God.) Marx and Lenin used an offshoot of it, Dialectical Materialism, as the intellectual base for Communism.

MITHRAISM: Described in "Major World Religions."

MODERNISM: Started in the 18th century. A movement aimed at infusing scientific and historical data into traditional Christianity. The Modernists emphasized the ethical aspects of Christianity rather than its speculation about creation and God. It was not well received by the church. Pope Pius X called it "the synthesis of all heresies. [2]

NATURAL RELIGION: Theologies which are developed from human reason and experience, not from supposedly miraculous or supernatural sources. Examples include Humanism and Agnosticism.

NIHILISM: Taken from the same Latin root as annihilate. Popularized by the Russian novelist Ivan Turgenev when he used the term to describe the hero in his novel "Fathers & Sons" in 1862. It started a significant philosophical movement in 19th & 20th century Russia. It denies any grounds for truth and moral principles. It also supports terrorism and destruction to correct a desperate situation.

ONTOLOGICAL ARGUMENT: The examination of the concept of God in an attempt to prove its existence. It argues that since people so readily believe in God, then God must exist.

ORIGINAL SIN: The classical Christian belief that the entire human race inherits the guilt of, and is punished for, Adam & Eve's act of disobedience. Since the first couple consumed the forbidden fruit, God, in his rage and disrespect for mankind, has decreed all humans are born evil and will go to hell unless they find salvation in his only son, Jesus Christ. Salvation cannot occur through any other religion. According to this doctrine, from the moment Adam & Eve were thrown out of the Garden of Eden, until Jesus started his ministry, (*a six to ten thousand year period,*) all people went to hell, no matter how good they were. (This decree was amended centuries later to not include the Hebrew Patriarchs, babies that had died and the handicapped.

PANTHEISM: This doctrine states that everything is made of and composed of God, including atoms. God doesn't just watch over us, etc., but *is* organic and inorganic matter.

PELAGIANISM: A "heretical" religious theory started by Pelagius, a British monk in the 5th century A. D. It states (1) Original Sin does not exist, so (2) there is no eternal damnation for unbaptized infants and (3) man can exercise freedom of choice about which religion to follow and can still go to heaven. Their conception of God was considered more gentle and forgiving as compared to God as defined by the then almighty Catholic Church. Many were persecuted for heresy.

POSITIVISM: Originated by Frenchman Auguste Comte in the 19th century and sometimes confused with Agnosticism. Its followers are uninterested in what isn't understandable, including God. It asserts that people should obtain knowledge more to describe and experience knowledge than to explain it. Positivism attempts to break everything down to analyzable units. They believe philosophy can serve a purpose but the only way to gain knowledge is from science. They had less interest in theology than agnostics. Also, the Positivists were mostly French while the agnostics were mostly English.

PROVIDENCE: The doctrine that God personally determines events throughout individual's lives with the fate God feels is best for each individual. Thus if you were disfigured in a car accident, Providence would assume God purposes planned events (or purposely did not stop events) so such a disfigurement would occur. Also it states God does this with mankind in general. This theory also asserts that if one believes in God, God will protect him or her, or a group, or even mankind, from harm. The belief in how much influence Providence has in one's life varies with each denomination, particularly in modern times. It's often associated with the theistic theory of "Predetermination."

ROMANTICISM: A movement created by European literature in the later 1700's and 1800's. There was an imaginative return to the Middle Ages and a preoccupation with mystery and superstition. It affected all of Europe, and to a lesser degree America.

SCIENTISM: Described in "Major World Religions."

SECULARISM: A school of thought initially presented by G. J. Holyoake (1817-1906) It states that morals, ethics and principles should be determined by the sociological development of the changing world around us. The divine origin of religious doctrines is doubted.

SECULAR CHRISTIANITY: An attempt to redevelop Christianity according to secular principles. Instead of the supernatural, the emphasis is on the world around us. Contemporary Agnosticism can be placed in this category.

SOPHISTS: Started in 5th century B.C. The Sophists are considered the first paid teachers of higher learning (professors) in the western world. They tended to be skeptics. They taught people how to be more successful in life. They also attempted to give others a better understanding of past philosophies. Many Sophists accumulated substantial wealth touring on the western world's first "lecture circuits."

STOICISM: School of thought founded in Greece by Zeno in 308 B.C. It was the most influential philosophy in the Roman Empire until Christianity took over. Stoics tended to fall back on principles preached by the earlier Greek Cynics. Nature, God, reason, fate and "Providence" were all part of the same force. Man is free to choose his own destiny and is not affected by a supernatural force. A wise, "Stoic" man would be free from outbursts of passion, joy or grief and would be submissive to and respectful of the laws of nature. Seneca is one of the most famous Stoics. (See "Other Notable People Related to Agnosticism.")

SUPERNATURAL: Something which exists, or is thought to exist even though it doesn't have an organic or inorganic nature (something such as a ghost.) It would be from a scientific standpoint, an invisible and unmeasurable force existing only in theory. God, gods and angels are also in this category.

THEISM: The belief in the infallible existence of one omnipotent and all knowledgeable creator (God) whose supernatural power transcends the universe. God is considered different, better and superior from everything else because God created everything else.

TRANSCENDENTAL: Some thing, concept or idea which is thought to exist but which we can't physically experience or touch, at least directly. The supernatural. God and metaphysics fall into this category. The transcendental is something which, at least at this point, can't be defined and classified by scientific methods.

TRANSCENDENTALISM: Originated by Henry David Thoreau and Ralph Waldo Emerson. States that everything represents God and thus everything is "divine." It denies the need for organized religion as everything already represents God. Attempts to improve yourself and the world around you are good because that improves what is "divine." Communes were started on this principle but didn't last.

UTILITARIANISM: The theological belief that the right and wrong of an action is determined by whether the outcome of the action is good or bad. The supreme good is whatever provides the greatest happiness to the greatest number of people.

ZOROASTRIANISM: Described in "Major World Religions".

Legal Notice: In this publication there may be inadvertent inaccuracies including technical inaccuracies, typographical inaccuracies and other possible inaccuracies. The writer and publisher of this publication expressly disclaim all liability for the use or interpretation by others of information contained in this publication and/or listed Web sites. The author, publisher and distributors of this publication hereby disclaim any and all liability for any loss or damage caused by errors or omissions, (should these exist) whether such errors or omissions resulted from negligence, accident, or other causes. If legal advice or other expert assistance is required, the services of a competent professional person in a consultation capacity should be sought. the information contained herein may be subject to varying state and/or local laws or regulations. All users are advised to retain competent counsel to determine what state and/or local laws or regulations may apply to the user's particular business. The Purchaser or Reader of this publication assumes responsibility for the use of these materials and information. Adherence to all applicable laws and regulations, federal, state, and local, governing professional licensing, business practices, advertising, and all other aspects of doing business in the United States or any other jurisdiction is the sole responsibility of the Purchaser or Reader. The Author and Publisher assume no responsibility or liability whatsoever on the behalf of any Purchaser or Reader of these materials. Any perceived slights of specific people or organizations are unintentional. Products, services and websites' content vary with time. Please verify any published information.

Absolutely Essential Tips For Buying & Selling On eBay

*eBay is a registered trademark of eBay Inc.

Copyright 2013

Table of Contents

BUYING ON EBAY

1) Last Minute Bidding Frenzies - Perhaps you've noticed that often there's a bidding frenzy in the last one minute of bidding. New bidders may suddenly start bidding in the hope that the previous bidders will not be watching or can't increase their bid in time. Often however it's because of *Sniping.*

Sniping websites automatically bid on your behalf, often in the last 10ish seconds. Simply sign up, enter an eBay item number and the maximum price you're willing to pay. Hidbid.com and goofbid.com offer sniping services that place bids for you.

Typically you'll need to give sniping sites your eBay password for them to work (ugh!!) Obviously that is a serious security concern.

There's little protection from eBay if things go wrong when sniping, since you willingly gave your password to a third party. If you do sign up for such a service, never use the same password for eBay as you use for other accounts like banks accounts or email addresses.

2) Second-chance Auction Scams, Beware of Them - Unscrupulous people sometimes watch bidders in high-dollar auctions and try to take unsuspecting buyer's money after an auction ends.

The scheme, known as a *Second-chance Auction Scam*, is just one of many types of Internet auction frauds reported to the *Internet Crime Complaint Center,* or *IC3*.

Second-chance scammers wait until auctions end and then offer bidders that lost, a phony second chance to purchase the item -- usually through a wire transfer service. This happens more often than people realize, beware!

3) Misspelling Search Tool - Typojoe.com, goofbid.com, bargainchecker.com, fatfingers.co.uk and baycrazy.com - There are many items listed on eBay every day that have misspelled words in the title. It's unfortunate for the seller but chances are good those listings will not come up well in eBay's search engine (because misspelling causes keyword problems) and thus not bring the seller top dollar. Their loss can be your gain!

4) Bidding Tip - Often sellers start auctions at .99 cents, (or at least under a dollar) hoping a bidding war will erupt. Many items go unspotted, staying at this super-low price (99 cents). *LastminuteAuction.com* hunts for eBay auctions due to finish within an hour but where the price still is very low.

With these items in particular, double-check delivery charges, as some sellers hope to recoup costs by charging a little extra (though eBay's now set maximum delivery charges for many categories).

5) Don't Forget About Facebook - *Facebook Marketplace* is a force to be reckoned with. Also sellers often are open to haggling. Just log on to your account at Facebook and search for "Marketplace". It's also worth checking to see if there's any local Facebook selling groups in your area.

6) Nigerian Type Scam for Paying. These unscrupulous people want to pay with a money order that they claim to already have handy. Often it's for more than the purchase amount. He writes to ask if the seller would be "honest enough" (or something of that nature) to send him the extra cash along with the item. (However he might just try to only buy the item with it and not ask for extra cash.) Unfortunately the money order can look okay but is counterfeit. They particularly like the *Buy It Now* feature.

7) Set Long-term Alerts For Rare Items - If you want something very specific or hard to find, set a 'favorite search' and eBay will email each time a seller lists your desired item.

Simply type a product in eBay's search bar, such as "silver dollar", and click 'save search'. Be as specific as possible for the most accurate results. When (and if) someone lists one, you're alerted with an email.

8) Don't Assume eBay's the Cheapest Place To Get Your Item - Many people assume that if it's on eBay, it's automatically the least expensive place to get it, but that often isn't the case. Perhaps you'd also like to use *shopbots* (shopping robots) that check numerous Internet retailers to find the best price. Type into a search engine "shopping comparison sites".

The same rule applies when buying used merchandise. Check used marketplaces on Amazon.com and Play.com - you may even get it for free on Freecycle or Freegle.

9) Check the eBay Going Rate For an Item - There's a quick way to check an eBay product's average price. Enter the item into the search box and click "completed listings". What will come up is a list of prices that similar auctions have already settled on. After that, sort it by "Price: lowest first". If the price is red, it means no one bought it. Green means it sold. Figure out the average price.

10) eBay has banned the selling of intangible items, and that includes curses! - Among the items that were prohibited as of August 30, 2012, are "advice; spells; curses; hexing; conjuring; magic; prayers; blessing services; magic potions; healing sessions; work from home businesses and information; wholesale lists, and drop shop lists."

11) Haggling on eBay Can Pay Off - There's nothing wrong with asking for a discount, even if the listing doesn't have the "make offer" indication. Haggling works best on *Buy It Now* listings, or auctions with a high start price and no bids. Also you'll likely do better if you haggle as the auction is coming closer to closing as the seller could start feeling more desperate.

To contact the seller, click on the seller's nickname then "ask seller a question". If you're polite, you'll likely get further. Blunt requests such as "dude, how about $15?" likely won't work out as well. Remember the seller is likely going to lose money doing this so no point in being annoying.

Once you've arranged a deal, try to keep the transaction within eBay. Ask the seller to add (or change) a Buy It Now price. That way you don't lose the usual eBay buyer protection privileges.

12) Other Things to Do To Exploit Sellers' Screw-ups - Some sellers make basic mistakes, leavings goods going for bargain money.

As well as spelling boo-boos, another error is to leave out key details such as shoe size, dress brand, saying a console's an a Wii when the photo shows a Xbox. At this point, many buyers give it up as "too much hassle".

So contact the seller to fill in gaps, but don't ask the question via the item's listing page, (because that way, when the seller replies, eBay lets them add their reply to the main listing, so it's no longer your secret.)

Instead, ask the question via the seller's profile (make it clear which item you're talking about). They might not bother with the extra hassle of adding it to the listing, so you'll be the only one in the know.

Also the seller might not realize how pricy an item he/she actually has.

13) Tool to Track Down Crazy End Times - Listings that finish at anti-social times often get fewer bids, thus sell for less. To locate auctions that finish when fewer people are around to bid on them, use BayCrazy's *Crazy End Time* search. (A lot more on the best times to end your auction in the next section of the book *"Selling on eBay"*.)

Check out their auto-bidding tools if you don't want to spend all that time in front of the computer bidding at odd times. Other BayCrazy.com tools include "unwanted gift" and "ending now" searches. www.baycrazy.com/search.php?page=nightowl (Baycrazy offers other eBay related opportunities also.)

14) Search Descriptions as Well as Titles - eBay automatically searches seller's titles for results that include your specified keywords. If you're not getting the results you want, try also searching the item's *description* too. (To do this go to Advanced Search.)

For example, imagine you were searching for a REI Jacket. Unfortunately the seller may be selling one but only put "Ski Jacket" in the title however he mentioned "REI" in the description. Include description in your search and then it should then come up.

15) Search Using eBay Boolean Logic - If a seller could describe an item different ways, you can make eBay search for several different ways of describing it at once. Just place "((" at the beginning and enter different phrases individually enclosed by quotation marks, then followed by commas.

So for example, type... (("fishing tackle", "hook", "reel" ...and it will simultaneously bring up listings that contain the words "fishing tackle", "hook" and/or "reel".

16) Add A Few Extra Cents to Your Bid - When bidding, you enter a "maximum bid", and eBay makes automatic bids on your behalf up to your maximum bid.

Don't enter a round number. For example, if a coat is currently selling for $20, and the most you are willing to pay for it is $25, enter a maximum bid of $25.24. If someone tries to outbid you by entering the round number of

$25, they will receive an outbid notice. eBay will go your bid, even though it's just 24 cents more.

17) Be Somewhat Skeptical of Feedback - eBay sellers have a feedback rating that acts as a useful guide to previous seller's opinion's of them. As a guideline, look for a seller with more than 98% positive feedback and a high feedback score of at least 30. Also ensure you read their feedback from their *selling*, not just their *buying*. (To see their feedback, click on their username).

18) Seller with Zero Feedback Could be Cause For Concern - Think twice before purchasing expensive items from a seller with zero feedback.

Remember feedback's useful but not infallible. One thing to watch for is traders selling a number of cheap things for $1ish each to build their feedback, and suddenly listing items costing hundreds each.

19) Check to Make Sure You're Bidding on the Actual Item - Sometimes you assume you're bidding for an item on eBay (or any auction site,) when all that's actually being sold is a link to another site selling it. People are not suppose to be able to sell these on eBay but they can fall through the cracks.

Always read the whole description in detail before bidding. Often the catch is hidden in the text at the end – an attempt to protect the seller from any recourse.

20) Scam - Beware of it - It's a red flag if a seller writes "Before bidding, contact me" then asks for a money transfer. Thieves who hijack actual eBay accounts might use this tactic.

21) Scam - Beware of it - Always be worried if you're asked to pay by an instant money transfer service such as Western Union or MoneyGram. Instant money transfer payments cannot be traced and are highly popular with thieves.

22) Sneakily Find Underpriced Buy It Nows - Feel free to hunt for Buy It Now bargains also. Perhaps the seller under-values their item making their price a good deal.

These steals are snapped up quickly. Go to "Advanced Search", select a category you're interested in, filter it to show *Buy It Now* items and sort the results.

23) Always Complain within 45 Days - Under eBay's buyer protection program, 45 days is the most number of days you have to open a case if you're unhappy with your purchase. (There are some exceptions such as tickets for events that are months away.) Read more on eBay's protection policy.
http://pages.ebay.com/help/policies/buyer-protection.html#conditions1

Under eBay's own Buyer Protection rules, buyers are eligible for a refund if the item's "not as described", meaning it didn't match the seller's description. http://pages.ebay.com/coverage/index.html

24) Pay by PayPal - Avoid sending checks and never use money orders. It's much harder for scammers to disappear with your cash when you use eBay's online payment system, PayPal.

Paying this way costs the same as paying by check, but means you're covered by eBay's Buyer Protection program. If an item is faulty, counterfeit or non-existent, you are far more likely to get a refund.

25) Outbid? Don't Give Up On It Yet - Missed out on a desired item by pennies? Don't give up hope. As every seller knows, sales sometimes don't materialize when buyers change their minds or can't come up with the dough. Because of that feel free to send a friendly message such as: "Hi, I've been looking for this poster for years and just saw your finished auction. Please let me know if the sale doesn't come through."

They may send a *Second-chance Offer*, which are sent out by sellers to unsuccessful bidders if the winner fails to pay up. Ask them to relist at an agreed *Buy It Now* price.

26) Know Your Consumer Rights - When buying from a person who makes or sells goods for resale on eBay you often have the same rights as when buying in person from a shop that does the same. This means your goods must be of satisfactory quality and as described.

With private sellers it's buyer beware. Buyers' only rights under law are that the product is fairly described and the owner has the right to sell it.

Under eBay's own Buyer Protection rules, buyers are eligible for a refund if the item is "not as described", meaning it doesn't match the seller's description.

27) Beware of All The Fakes - While eBay has a 'flag and remove' policy to help identify fakes, still plenty fall through the cracks.

If you're buying big-name brands, do your research first. Carefully check sellers' feedback and post on the forum's eBay board to get others' opinions. Be especially wary of overseas sellers or branded items that seem especially cheap.

The more *unprofessional* the photos, likely the better. Thieves often take professional photos from the brands' sites. Legitimate sellers typically take photos of items at home that might not come out as well.

28) Think Twice Before You Give A Seller Negative Feedback - Of course, negative feedback is often justified but have a heart, don't leave negative or even *neutral* feedback without first trying to work the issue out with the seller. Most sellers are good folks who will try to help particularly, as it can mean a lot to their business to stay in your good graces.

Remember eBay users can view the feedback you've left for others, and if you leave a significant amount of negative feedback, they may well decide you're too high of a risk to sell to.

29) Add An Item You're Interested in to eBay's "Watch List" - Want to keep track of an item without bidding on it? eBay lets you add items to a "Watch List", so you can relax knowing you'll get an email reminder within 36 hours of the auction ending. To watch an item, just click the "*add to watch list*" link in the upper part of the item's eBay webpage.

30) Don't Do Private Purchasing - Sellers may suggest you do a deal outside eBay for a cheaper price. If you do you'll likely have less protection if things go bad. You won't be able to leave negative feedback and you won't be protected by eBay's Buyer Protection Plan.

31) Think Safety When Picking Up An Item In Person - The usual precautions apply. If you get to their door and the seller's holding a butcher knife, now's the time to run.

32) Think International - There's bargains to be had on overseas eBay sites. To include foreign auctions in search results, click "worldwide" for location.

Still can't find what you want? Another option is buying directly from *international* eBay sites. The main ones are USA, Canada, Australia, Germany, France and Spain - there's a full list at the bottom of eBay's homepage. Make sure that the item reads *"Shipping to: worldwide"* before bidding as some international sellers only do business with their country's buyers.

Always factor in postage and if applicable, custom fees. Remember that return postage fees could be hefty.

Also what kind of credit card protections will there be? You're often still protected by eBay and PayPal's buyer protections (if you use PayPal), but it's worth investigating. Type in "buyer protection" in PayPal.

33) Don't Forget The Online Classified Ads - Again, let's not assume that because it's on eBay, that's where you'll get the best price for an item. Unfortunately that's often just not the case. Type "top classified ad sites" or something of that nature, into search engines. There's also *Freecycle* and *Freegle*. (Those two sites offer free stuff. freecycle.org and ilovefreegle.org.)

Remember, anyone can post on these classified ad sites. If someone asks you to pay by MoneyGram or Western Union, as always be concerned. It's a bad way to pay.

34) Check Other Auction Sites Also - There are other auction sites that can be found through search engines. If you're searching for something specific, it's also worth adding it to your search. *Auctionlotwatch*.com is a useful shopbot for online auctions. Search for an item and it trawls the big auction sites for you.

35) Check Cashback and Voucher Websites - Check cashback websites to see if there's money back available on your eBay purchase. Type into search engines: "cashback and voucher sites".

Cashback sites give you a cut of their proceeds by setting you up with product and/or service providers.

36) eBay has trained teachers that could be in your area. Also see eBay University. Check out:
http://pages.ebay.com/sellerinformation/howtosell/university.html

Selling on eBay

1) Join eBay Forums - Ask questions about anything, selling, buying etc. Great information is posted already and could be of use. Work together as a team. Find eBay and other auction forums by looking those up in search engines. Ebay has forums also. http://forums.ebay.com/category/Ebay-Discussion-Boards/2001

2) eBay Research Tool 1 - To help in your research about selling items, you can go Type into a search engine "best selling eBay items." EBay provides that information.

3) eBay Research Tool 2 - You can use Ebuyers (www.ebuyersedge.com) to just search eBay for items as well as set up a saved eBay search (or a number of them). You'll get alerted with an e-mail when a matching item is listed.

4) Sell Refurbished Products - Refurbished products fall somewhere in between new and used products. Refurbished products are not new, but often they aren't significantly used either. Sometimes a customer buys the product and for whatever reason, returns it for a refund. The item is then returned to the manufacturer, given an inspection, repaired as necessary and sold as refurbished.

There are various ways an item can become refurbished.

1. The packaging of an item can be damaged during shipping. In that case the item is sent back to the seller/manufacturer. Refurbished items usually come with manufacturer's warranties. Although sometimes the warranties that come with refurbished items are for a shorter period of time, the products are usually in very good condition.

2. Items that have a slight defect or flaw, like a scratch or mechanical flaw, might be returned to the manufacturer. The manufacturer repairs the items, repackages them and marks them refurbished.

3. Demonstration units are also considered refurbished, but generally that's when they're returned to the manufacturer, inspected and repackaged.

4. Brand new overstock items can also be marked refurbished.

5. Sometimes it's a situation where only the packaging of an item is opened. It's re-packaged or even just closed up and marked as refurbished.

Refurbished Products Advantages:

a. Refurbished products are significantly cheaper than new products. They also come with warranties, boxes and everything else new products come with.

b. Selling refurbished products is more profitable, even though refurbished products cost significantly less than new products. On eBay (and at other places) refurbished products can sell for the same price as new ones. (Many people buy refurbished products thinking they're buying new ones.)

c. Refurbished products are sometimes new! When you buy a lot of refurbished products they might actually be overstock items or factory overruns. In that case you would be buying new products at a fraction of the price.

Refurbished Products Disadvantages:

a. Refurbished is not new, even though refurbished products can be exactly the same as new ones, people simply prefer new items.

b. Refurbished products are sometimes the previous year's models. If you're selling electronics or computers it could bring the selling prices down.

5) Finding Products To Sell - Unfortunately finding products to sell can be the toughest part of starting your eBay business. Many people end up opting against starting an eBay business because they can't find a good supplier.

a) YELLOWPAGES.COM - www.yellowpages.com. Try this first. Yellowpages.com can find specialized suppliers in your area. Type in "wholesale" into the search box and you will be given a bunch of subdirectories to further explore. Make sure the search is based on a location near you. Next type "wholesale directory" or "wholesale directories" into search engines.

When searching also try inputting keywords such as overstock, salvage, surplus, liquidation, auction, refurbished, refurb, supplier, closeout, wholesale, etc.

b) BUY FROM AN ACTUAL EBAY SELLER. Buy multiple items and get a discount. That discount could be your margin of profit.

c) BUY WHOLESALE LOTS FROM EBAY AND RESALE THEM - Go to eBay and search for "wholesale lot". If you buy a big lot, you could find you profit best by individually selling the items in the big lot.

d) PERHAPS SELL DIGITAL COUPONS. You should be able to get them for free. As of this writing, people are posting that coupons sell well on eBay. If you're selling coupons, you need to mention that your auction is for the time you spend finding, assembling (sorting) and sending the coupons to the buyer rather than selling the coupons themselves. It's illegal to sell coupons and that's why auctions say the payment is for the time to gather and sort them. Still it can take time to find good coupons and first folks need to know where to look.

e) BUY FROM LIQUIDATION COMPANIES - A liquidator is someone that buys overruns from big retailers (Sears, K-mart, Wal-Mart etc.) at a fraction of the wholesale price. Sometimes big stores can't sell everything they have. The stuff they couldn't sell needs to be gotten rid of as soon as possible to make room for new products. This is where liquidation companies come in. They buy the overruns products, often at a fraction of the wholesale price. When a liquidation company buys a couple of truckloads full of overruns, the next thing it must do is sell these overruns ASAP to make room for more overruns. Since the liquidator must get rid of the products as soon as possible, the products are sold at cheap prices and often in bulk. Perhaps there are liquidator stores in your town what would make you a deal and you wouldn't necessarily have to buy in bulk.

f) EBOOK SALES - With ebooks, you can sell a digital product that can simply be emailed to your customer. No packing and shipping involved! Selling ebooks on eBay is easy. In fact there are systems you can implement to essentially automate the entire process. You could do a *Buy It Now* auction, or just start the bidding at a reasonable price. When the auction ends and the buyer pays you, all you need to do is email the eBook to them. Again, that's the great thing about downloadable information products: no packaging or shipping is necessary. Perhaps you'd like to offer an entire collection of eBooks to sell on eBay. You'll need eBooks that you own or have given you resale rights.

g) You can sell peoples' houses, cars, boats, or even jewelry collections. Just look in the for sale listings of your local newspaper and look at all of the great stuff for sale that would sell on eBay. Call up the owners of the items advertised in the newspaper and offer to sell the stuff for them. Looking for stuff in newspapers is great because the people that are using a newspaper to sell something probably know little about eBay and are desperate to get rid of the stuff they're advertising. These people are also the ones that are willing to lower the price and haggle, and that is great because the lower the price they are willing to let the item go for, the more profit you can make by selling their stuff.

h) RUNNING ADS TO FIND MERCHANDISE - You can run ads in print media and/or post what you're looking for in Internet forums with something like "I will buy your stuff". As previously noted, if you are going to use this method you will need to pick a used product that keeps its value well. If you're going to use this method you should buy things like jewelry and watches, antiques and other things that appreciate with age.

A previous seller's success story was selling old collectable Apple computers. This is a type of item that some people have laying around in the basement or attic, and will likely never use again. They're more than happy to unload it and get a little money for it at the same time. But on eBay it was a whole new ballgame. There are thousands of people who collect old collectable computers.

6) Sell To Resellers - Anyone looking to buy products and resell them to make a profit is a very good customer that will come back and buy from you again and again. Plenty of people buy stuff on eBay then resell it on eBay! There are also those who buy products on eBay to resell them on their other ecommerce websites or actual stores they may own. A lot of PowerSellers (special higher volume eBay sellers with a closer relationship to eBay) started by buying stuff off of eBay and simply putting it back up for auction.

7) Order Samples If Possible - This is a particularly good tip if you don't have a chance to inspect and see the products you are ordering in person. Many people starting out on eBay make the mistake of placing a big order before actually seeing what they're ordering. By ordering samples you'll be able to test not only the quality of the products you're ordering but the service, communication and legitimacy of the company you're ordering from. If you're thinking of selling designer clothing on eBay, be extra careful when ordering your supplies from the Internet. There is a lot of fake (counterfeit) clothing being sold on the Internet. Remember the pictures on the supplier's website may look real, but that doesn't mean they will be sending you what's in the picture.

If you find a great deal but the "supplier" won't allow any sample orders and wants you to pay through an untraceable method, be wary.

8) Second-chance Offers - If the buyer of your item falls through, you can send the other bidders a *Second-chance Offer* to see if they're still interested in buying it.

9) The Listing's Title - The title of your listing should be clear, relevant to what you are selling and attention grabbing. Always include the correct spelling of the item in the title. Don't try to make the title "cool" by deliberately misspelling words, unless perhaps if the slang name for it is popular. If you misspell the title, your listing won't show up in search results because presumably most people aren't searching for the slang name (or misspelled version) of the product.

The title has to be short (eBay rules), so make sure you include the name of the item and abbreviated descriptions, and try not to waste any space on words that are not needed. *By the same token, always use the entire allotted space to write your title. In general, the longer the title, the better, as long as all your keywords are relevant.*

10) Keywords & Relevancy - Make sure the brand name of what you're selling is in the title! If you're selling a Champion Portable Generator, your listing title should include the make and model number, in this case "New Champion 42431 Portable Generator, 1500 Watt". Your listing title should be a short, abbreviated description of the item you are selling.

The name of the product in the title has to do with the search results (keywords). If people want to buy your portable generator they may search "portable generator, generator, Champion, Champion portable generator," etc. You want to make your listing show up in as many search results as possible.

In review, a wild but catchy title will definitely grab the attention of most people who see it, but won't come up in many people's search results, unless also in the title listing is the name of the product that people would type in when looking for it. (Even that's not guaranteed to work.)

11) If a potential customer wants other people's opinions on a product you sell, you might want to send them to the Amazon.com's webpage for the site as Amazon posts feedback from buyers of that same product. Make sure that Amazon is not selling it for less than you are or that idea could backfire!

12) Mention Flaws: If there is a flaw in the item you are selling, make sure you mention it (though try to call it something else like "scratch" or "mark" if that's what it is.) If your product has a flaw and you don't mention it in your listing, you could get negative feedback and a request for a refund from the person who buys the "flawed" item.

If possible, make the flaw sound positive. You could say "this product has a small dent that has no effects on its operation, but because of this you save big bucks!"

Mentioning a flaw also can make you look like an honest person. You can even have the flaw mentioned in your bullet points - Small scratch on the top (saves you money!!)

13) Host Your Own Pictures - You can host your own pictures on another website or your eBay Store and thus show many, many more photos free of charge.

14) Payment Options: - You should offer the customer several different choices of payment. Most of your customers will pay you through PayPal, (PayPal is owned by eBay,) so make sure you get a PayPal account (www.PayPal.com). Of course, not everyone who buys items on eBay prefers PayPal, some may prefer Western union's Bidpay or another payment system. Another one you should sign up for is StormPay as it can be used by people in some countries where PayPal is not used or as popular. For your free StormPay account go to: stormpay.com.

Wire Transfers - Unscrupulous overseas buyers prefer these as they're not as traceable. It's preferable not to take them.

15) Offering SquareTrade Warranties - If applicable to what you're selling, another good way to build trust is to sign up for SquareTrade warranties at www.squaretrade.com. www.squaretrade.com/seller-faq

16) About Me Page - The About Me page is often overlooked by many eBay sellers (and buyers.) While having the free About Me page likely will not dramatically increase your sales, it can help if you have good things to say about yourself and a nice picture. Note, many sellers only include links to their listings and maybe not enough information about themselves in the About Me page.

17) People Bidding with 0 Feedback ratings - Having a good to great feedback rating is so important as you know. Many sellers refuse letting members with 0 feedback bid on their auctions. Getting a negative feedback from somebody that unpredictable is simply a risk we don't want to take. In many cases, we simply don't trust them.

18) Best Time To End Your Auction - The best time for an auction to close (end) is in the evenings and on weekends as that's when most people are on the Internet for that type of activity! You want to make sure that when your auction is closing (ending), everyone that's interested in it is available to bid on it. The mornings are the times that the eBay website gets the least visitors (as people are more often sleeping or working.)

If you live in the Eastern Time Zone, list your auction between 9pm-11pm, Central Time Zone list between 8-10pm, Mountain Time Zone between 7-9pm, and for the Pacific Time Zone list between 6-8pm. This will give you the biggest exposure at the end of your auction. The debate is out as to what day your auction should end on. Some sellers report that Tuesday, Wednesday and Thursday are best. Other sellers report that Saturday and Sunday are best.

There are a few exceptions though. For example, some business products sell best during weekdays and during work hours. Obviously this is because people are usually ordering those types of products at work, for work. Studies have shown that a listing that ends at peak hours can attract up to 25% more bids than one that ends in non-peak hours. Listing your auctions at optimal times is one of the easiest ways to attract more bids.

To end the auction in the evenings, you'll need to put the item for sale in the evening (*or use listing software [see next page] to do it for you*) as eBay considers each day to have a length of 24 hours.

Note, it's eBay's practice that when someone's auction is ending, that listing shows up higher on keyword search results (which is a good thing!)

19) Terms of Service Webpage (Yours) - That's something even a lot of experienced sellers don't seem to include, though it likely won't be necessary if all the information is already in your FAQ webpage. For instance, what's the return policy? What are the shipping options, and what will they cost? What are the accepted methods of payment? How soon is payment to be sent? What is the warranty?

20) Listing Software (For Your Items) - Listing software organizes your eBay listings making the listing part of your business simpler and more efficient. There are many different kinds of listing software. You can do an Internet search for them.

Turbo Lister is free software from eBay. Turbo Lister allows you to upload thousands of listings at a time. It saves listings, schedules your listings and uploads them to eBay automatically. Using it you can edit multiple listings at the same time, preview what your listings will look like before uploading them and more. More eBay software is offered at: http://pages.ebay.com/help/sell/advanced_selling_tools.html

21) Drop Shipping What You Sell - With drop shipping all you have to do is list items up for auction and when they sell, you contact your supplier, who ships the products from their factory, straight to your customers. In theory drop shipping is a good way to go, but it could offer problems. What happens when you sell items and your supplier sends them to the wrong addresses? What happens when you sell items and your supplier is out of stock? In those cases your reputation suffers. If you are going to use drop shipping; make sure there is good communication between you and your supplier (drop shipper.) Also make sure you have some products in stock in case the supplier runs out by the time your auctions have closed.

22) eBay Stores - eBay stores can be great if you have a number of items to sell. First you'll need to reach the minimum number of feedbacks required (10) to open one. Most PowerSellers have eBay stores. Store sellers can see an increase in profit of up to 25% in the first three months of opening the store (according to eBay). Having your own eBay store can save you a substantial amount of money in listing fees and let you sell items in a fixed price format as well as selling via auctions. Also you can list items for a much longer time and store them in your inventory list for 30, 60, 90, 120 days and even "Good till Cancelled". You'll can feature links to other auctions in all your listings by utilizing a cross promotion tool. There are also bonuses like your own search engine and monthly reports from eBay featuring statistics and dada about your sales in the past month.

An eBay store also gives you a location. It gives you a base of operation, a place where people can easily find you, and a place where repeat customers can come back to. Your customers will be able to bookmark and return to your store, and it may also be indexed in the major search engines. So if you're selling silver dollars, and someone does a BING search for silver dollars, your eBay store may appear in the results along with the usual online retail websites! Obviously this can increase your traffic greatly, and likewise boost your sales.

23) Your eBay Store Identity - Ideally your eBay store should look different from your competition. You can use the design templates eBay offer you, but perhaps it's best to use original graphics. Fortunately eBay Stores are customizable. Ideally, to establish your name, your eBay store should appear like your listings as much as possible. Same colors, design and look.

24) Get a Domain Name - You need to get a simple and memorable domain name. A domain name makes it simple for people to find you. The standard web address eBay will give to your store will look like this: *stores.ebay.com/yourname*, this is not a very memorable web address and it's too long to be easy to type into a web browser. It would be best if you had a web address like *mystore.com*.

End

The Absolutely Essential Guide to Understanding Elder Financial Abuse

By Winston Phillips

Copyright (C) 2013

Table of Contents

1. Introduction

** Elder Americans were robbed of an estimated **$2.9 billion in 2011**, up 12 percent from 2008, according to a MetLife Mature Market Institute study.*

* Kathleen Quinn, executive director of the National Adult Protective Services Association: "Seniors who lose their money are more likely to go into a nursing home, die or go on Medicaid. This is a huge fiscal drain on Medicare and Medicaid. If we can prevent financial abuse or intervene early enough to save the money that remains, then that will save Medicare and especially Medicaid tons of money."

* According to the National Center on Elder Abuse, only one in 14 cases of abuse is actually reported. (2009 statement.)

* "Once an older adult has been ripped off, he or she is likely to succumb to other fraudulent financial schemes," according to Prescott Cole, an attorney with the Coalition to End Elder Financial Abuse (CEASE). "They will run into more and more of these kinds of scams and they will fall into each and every one of them" Cole said.

* National Adult Protective Services Association is an organization representing adult protective service (APS) workers, who are responsible for investigating abuse, neglect and exploitation of adults who are elderly or have disabilities. APS workers will go directly into victim's or potential victims' homes. Kathleen Quinn, executive director of the National Adult Protective Services Association notes.

* In 2010, Investor Protection Trust estimated 7.3 million older adults – 20 percent of older Americans, have been victimized by financial abuse. Most that commit financial elder abuse are people who have already gained their victim's trust the report notes.

* On average, more women than men are victimized according to the National Adult Protective Services Association (NAPSA). The typical victim of elder financial abuse is between the ages of 70 and 89, female, frail, Caucasian and at least to a degree, impaired mentally. She is overly trusting of others and may be feel isolated and lonely.

* (A) Research by the University of Iowa found that 35 to 40 percent of community-dwelling older adults performed poorly on measures related to decision-making ability. (B) Poor decision-makers are more likely to

become victims of deceptive advertising. (Conclusion of a study by Natalie Denburg et al.)

(Many of the above quotes, statistics and points were in the article: "Elder Financial Abuse Estimated at $2.9 Billion a Year" - By Bill Benson and Nancy Aldrich - The Sentinel - November, 2011 - Health Benefits ABCs - www.smpresource.org.)

Definition: Elder financial abuse is the illegal taking, misuse or concealment of funds, property or assets of a vulnerable elder at risk for harm by another due to changes in physical functioning, mental functioning or both. (National Center on Elder Abuse [NCEA]).

Definition: "Elder Abuse is a single or repeated act, or lack of appropriate action, occurring in any relationship where there is an expectation of trust that causes harm or distress to an older person". (WHO)

By cruising senior citizen facilities, or meeting seniors in other ways, predators can have a much higher payday than many other crimes. Also, the predator probably can make it look like the money or property was gifted to them, thus they'll claim no crime was committed.

Hello, what you're going to read is a true story. Sadly my elderly father's net worth was wiped out. He would unexpectedly find himself in debt. There likely would be no significant inheritance for the kids and grandkids, and the pain and suffering he and others felt (and continue to feel) would be immense.

There are a number of factors that can open up a senior citizen to financial abuse, in this case catastrophic financial abuse. If a romantic relationship is occurring, whether it's heterosexual or homosexual, often there are changes in emotions that can make one of them more responsive to the demands of the other. That includes letting one's guard down financially, and/or becoming unreasonably generous. There is also dealing with the blackmail, if it occurs.

I have purposely kept this book short and easy to read so the general public can perhaps more readily understand how surprisingly often financial abuse of the elderly occurs and how important it is for you to recognize financial elder abuse in its early stages.

Please also note that it's likely illegal in your state to not report elder abuse to authorities.

On a side note, the electricity used to write this book was almost entirely provided by solar panels.

2. Overview

There is a very real risk that lurks for senior citizens. My family found out the hard way, and don't think you're too smart to see it coming as there were a surprisingly high number of people that this predator of the elderly fooled in regard to this event.

Hello, my father was a catastrophic victim of a senior citizen financial predator and it can happen to an elder in your family, particularly if they are living alone. The predator saw opportunity in my financially secure recently widowed father's desire for, among other things, adventure, interest in having someone to drive him around, help him do errands, and be a general go-to guy. Unfortunately my father's appreciation and affection towards the predator would help cause him to lower his guard in regard to protecting his savings.

It was a disaster for the family. In a matter of months my father suddenly found himself without his nest egg (a small 6 figure sum) and in debt. The predator had also quietly maxed out my father's credit cards. My future also turned very cloudy due to this event. It changed my life dramatically. Money I was expecting to get for having worked for my father, I was now never likely to get. The debt I had taken on in expectation of this revenue was substantial. I was jobless and broke with my credit cards almost completely maxed out. My father's financial security was no longer there for any of his kids to fall back on. And that would be only part of the long gut-wrenching aftermath of this tragedy.

Now before we go further I'll admit the obvious, my father had his trust terribly abused and there was a great deal of naivety involved. As part of this disaster he had not only endured extensive identity theft, but had given the predator money, as well as paid for activities, some pricy, that they had done together.

When others, including family members, asked him if he was giving money to the predator, he said no, but he was and/or would be. When others around him voiced concern about him being with who turned out to be a financial predator, alarm bells didn't go off for him. He had personality changes as well. He was more of a kid again and was having fun. He got more combative and confident, even healthier. Unfortunately his more confident, aggressive nature would be a problem as people, who would have ordinarily been more aggressive in questioning his relationship with the predator, became less inclined to question his actions. That unfortunately included me.

As one of his offspring, I respected his opinion more than almost anybody as he is my father, he spoke with confidence and previously I could usually count on him to give me great advice.

Sadly, so impressed was he by the apparent financial prowess of this predator that he would eventually let the man have significant control over his finances. My father would not regularly and/or adequately monitor his monthly credit card statements. This is one of the holy grails for the economic predator of the elderly.

The police are typically not under any obligation to keep tabs on repeat offender senior citizen predators such as this one (unlike sex offenders). Where budget cuts are severe, the situation is even worse.

Unless one is well off financially, there is life before, and after the disaster's discovery. Nothing would ever be the same.

After becoming aware of the terrible misfortune, children and friends of the victim feel the shame and frustration of not having done more to alert and/or better coach the victim, though in this case, concern was voiced by a significant number of people, but for the most part it was ignored.

My father was victimized by a repeat offender and sadly information on this predator to that nature was online if one looked hard enough and knew the guy's full name. One friend of my father's saw this information about the predator weeks before this disaster became known.

Unfortunately she never even mentioned it to my father. Had she made him aware of it, as much as 40 percent of his net worth could have been saved (not to mention all those weeks' worth of fraudulent credit card purchases.)

3. The Aftermath

The pain and suffering this caused my father can't be understated.

There is the emotional shock for all. There are the frantic phone calls to financial institutions, visiting of one or more lawyers, the police interview(s), desperately trying to get a hold of the predator and more.
Incidentally, watch out for the tricks the predator plays after the event in an attempt to legally deflect blame.

Due to their lowered energy level, diminished mental facilities and/or depression caused by the event, many senior citizens lack the energy to try whole-heartedly to reclaim as much of the debt as possible. There are those that simply lose the will to live. The clean-up and recovery work will often end up becoming the kid's and/or other's responsibility (and that can include financial responsibility.) Partial recovery can take years, assuming it's even successful.

Important: Make sure the predator didn't get the victim to make a whole new will and testament and/or get the victim to give the predator power of attorney. Unfortunately the victim may not even know.

There are those that will search for the predator and try to strong arm him/her into repaying the debt, assuming he can be found.

Everybody blames the kids, particularly if anyone of them lived in the same town and/or was around the victim and predator when they were together. If people benefitted in some way from favors given to them by the predator, then they can feel even more frustration.

To make him feel better, the victim likely will be told by others that the kids should have done more to warn him or her of possible impending misfortune. Also the victim could himself deflect the blame for what occurred by blaming the kid(s) (and/or others) for not being more suspicious and involved. **That in and of itself is good reason for offspring to investigate a potential predator as early as possible as this is just another way the kids will suffer later on.**

Of course most everybody else thinks that if they were the kids, or other close relatives, they would have seen what was transpiring and would have stopped it. That may or may not be true. But once again the kids are blamed, this time for also being naive and too trusting of their father's judgment. This is particularly true as therapists often use this argument in the healing process.

Such a victimization is a terrible blow to anybody but perhaps more so late in life. There is a grieving process associated with the recovery. As finances suddenly become so tight, there are other changes in life. The victim may have to move to cheaper living quarters, give up his more expensive drugs. For months perhaps he'll have to borrow money to catch up on his bills.

Relatives could blame each other for years to come and old hostilities could re-surface, scarring relationships for life. On the other hand, a major crisis like this can bring people together again after long absences.

One family member may now get the only power of attorney and in the future that could lead to problems for one or more other family members.

Another blow to you could be that in retrospect you realize that your senior citizen family member may have already had some significant to serious mental health issues that you misjudged or chose to previously ignore thinking "he was always a bit of a character" or something of that nature. Depending on how much money was stolen through identity theft and/or how much he gave the predator and/or spent on him or her, it will become apparent how, for perhaps a surprisingly long period of time, the future financial needs of his/her kids and grandkids took a backseat to his predatory lover/friend. That is something the family members have to deal with for the rest of their lives. The victim likely will realize his mistake, feel terrible about it and will apologize for losing the family money, but how much good does that do, especially since it's the kids or other relatives that will have to do so much in helping him clean up the mess, and likely for years to come, including perhaps after his passing away.

Because of such a savage attack, the victim may lose, at least for a while, the will to live, or live with any great conviction. There will very likely be significant changes to their personality. With the depression can come anger and he may become short-tempered and/or develop issues that make him difficult to be around, at least at times. The victim could change his will based on how relatives act after the loss comes to light. In-fighting among relatives could last a lifetime.

4. Warning Signs That a Senior Citizen Could Be (and/or is being) Financially Taken Advantage Of

Statistically women are victims in larger numbers than men. Many cases of elder financial abuse are caused by relatives, close friends and caregivers. In that case it may be tougher to recognize that it's happening, at least early on, as you might expect to see them together and interacting a lot. (Of course we all know about people tricking seniors into paying many thousands more for something than was reasonable. That is further discussed in a section further on.)

Seniors might be more trusting if somebody is nice to them, especially if they are lonely and in need of the attention. A senior may be impressed by, and envious of, the younger person's stamina and/or good looks. All this often is magnified when the senior is isolated.

Please also note that it's likely illegal in your state to not report elder abuse to authorities.

Cindy Hounsell, head of the Women's Institute for a Secure Retirement (WISER) and the Administration on Aging's National Education and Resource Center on Women and Retirement, identifies the following warning signs to watch for in older adults:

1. Taking a large amount out of the bank or other cash accounts
2. Making numerous withdrawals of smaller amounts – say, $100 at a time
3. Writing a large check to someone they do not know
4. Changing power of attorney or beneficiaries on insurance or investment accounts
5. Bouncing checks or bills going unpaid when there should be enough money to cover bills
6. Making unusual or unnecessary purchases – golf clubs or jewelry
7. Agreeing to make unnecessary home repairs – new siding on the house
8. Becoming too close with a much younger person or an inappropriate person
9. Having a caregiver that is too interested in her finances.*

(From the article: "Elder Financial Abuse Estimated at $2.9 Billion a Year" – By Bill Benson and Nancy Aldrich – The Sentinel – November 2011 – Health Benefits ABCs – www.smpresource.org.)

I'd like to provide the following additional list. Sorry for any redundancies with the previous list. As is obvious, what can happen on these lists can happen in the natural course of events in life. They're simply being suggested as possible reasons for serious concern. (*The following is not necessarily in order of importance as certain suggestions may be more applicable to your case than others*):

1. When you need to get money from him or her, does your senior citizen relative have you talk to the potential predator to get it? That likely means he's giving the predator money and/or access to his/her money.

2. He/she is giving this potential predator their credit/charge card (or related other financial information) to use.

3. Has your elder previously gone through a long term high stress event like taking care of a dying spouse? Has it happened in the last 0-3 years? Their judgment and/or personality could have suffered from this trauma.

4. Your elder is selling off assets for less than logical reasons, particularly if she/he doesn't want to talk about it, but beware, the predator's influence could make him lie to you.

5. He doesn't want to live with any family members or other old friends so he's free to develop possibly questionable relationship(s) while not under their scrutiny.

6. Your relative hates financial bookkeeping (perhaps including balancing a checkbook) and didn't do it that often throughout his/her life. Perhaps someone else, particularly their spouse, had dealt with the family finances throughout most of their life.

7. You have noticed that the potential predator uses items without permission and/or is misleading to get money.

8. He or she had a very long relationship where their partner (typically their spouse) was the dominant person and he/she was the more submissive person.

9. Does the potential predator seem nervous around relatives of the potential victim and/or others that could see through his/her motives, unlike the senior citizen?

10. Does the potential predator talk about jail, probation or related things like there is a familiarity there?

11. Does the potential victim heap praise on the potential predator that is beyond the norm? This could be a sign that the potential victim's judgment is being compromised. It could also be a sign of a romance.

12. His "friend" has unexpectedly changed his attitude and become more hostile toward your senior citizen and/or others around your elder. That is how the predator to my father became later on in their relationship. By then my father had little or no money left for the predator to steal.

13. The senior citizen prefers to hang out with a person or people that are significantly younger than him or her. The younger they are, the more concerned you might want to be.

14. He or she is mad at their kin. and not particularly concerned if he leaves money to his kids or others.

15. Don't assume that a caregiver has been adequately vetted. One of the benefits a caregiver might get in life is that sometimes they get put in the will or get money or property from who they are caring for.

16. As a predator's specialty could be to go after gay, or gay curious senior citizens (and many do), is your senior citizen showing signs of homosexual interest? Many in this category gravitate to younger, more aggressive, better looking males or females. This should particularly be a concern if they are re-discovering or developing, for the first time, their homosexual/bisexual side. Great lengths could be gone through to hide this.

17. Does your elder live in a U.S. state that has more relaxed laws against elder abuse? Predators often prefer living in those states.

18. Is he/she weak emotionally? He/she may not act that way with you but how about with others? Emotionally weak people are among the predator's favorite prey.

19. Does the potential predator have an unrealistic amount of drama in his or her life? A certain amount of it the potential predator could be making up.

20. The web sites your senior citizen goes to and/or literature he has, can tell you something. Often he'll try to hide these if they can be incriminating.

21. Keep an eye on the new people he meets, including the clubs he joins (but remember we can readily misjudge situations).

22. He has become more confident and aggressive since meeting this potential predator and less interested in other's criticism of the potential predator.

23. He or she is not particularly bright to start out with.

24. Does he or she feel lost, depressed and/or abandoned? A senior who has lost a spouse, his old friends, siblings and others may be more willing to put up with a dysfunctional or abusive relationship thinking it's better than nothing at all. Emotional blackmail might be attempted, such as, "You'll never see me again if you don't give me that money." Or "Give me it or you'll never see your grandkids again."

25. The drug, or drugs he takes are making him more vulnerable.

26. He is desperate for someone to drive him around and help him do his normal activities.

27. The extended or long-term care facility he or she resides at does not actively monitor potential senior citizen predators who may frequent their establishment. (They may claim they do though.)

28. Males can be more adventurous than females and their paternal nature could be less conducive than the maternal instinct of females in the preservation of money for family use.

29. Is your senior citizen getting prices and bids on construction related work, a topic that she/he is not familiar with? In that case there's an increased chance of being overcharged.

5. Financial Abuse of Elders Caused by Romantic Relationships

There are very real potential risks that lurk for senior citizens of any sexual orientation. The warning signs previously listed in this book are also applicable when it comes to romance. Many women are victimized in this manner. My suggestion however is to be especially vigilant when it comes to homosexual relationships. A senior citizen's search for homosexual fulfillment can help make him/her a target for a predator and beware, a predator's specialty could be going after gay, or gay curious senior citizens. Remember, predators tend to be people that will do whatever it takes.

Also as the police might go under the assumption that a romantic relationship of some sort was part of the equation, it could become more difficult to charge the predator as the predator would claim the stolen money was gifted to him or her by their lover.

Often there are changes in emotions that occur in people when in special relationships, even for a short time. These can make one person more responsive to the demands of the other. That includes letting our guard down financially, and/or being unreasonably generous. There is also dealing with the blackmail, if it occurs.

Incidentally I wanted to note the obvious, that many senior citizens experience the gay lifestyle and have none of the problems discussed in this book (particularly if they have been doing it for many years.) From my research however, it appears that there's a particularly high risk if the senior citizen is just now exploring, or re-discovering, his or her homosexuality/bisexuality. Women need to be very vigilant about this as it's in the female nature to romantically gravitate toward confident aggressive men. Case studies however show that this includes a disproportionately high number of predators.

Of course younger women going after older men to benefit financially is perhaps a better known form of sexual senior citizen exploitation, though in various ways it's considered socially acceptable. Did the woman get him to pay a big debt of hers or of a family member of hers? That may or may not be legal.

How about the romance of two of the same generation where all of a sudden your senior citizen has bought her a car or house and it's in her name? That may or may not be legal.

6. Financial Abuse Committed by Relatives, Close Friends and Caregivers

The basic points laid out in this book are just as pertinent in this category. This book covers all types of elder financial abuse in broad strokes. There is a great deal already written in other books about this category as it likely contains the people that cause the most financial abuse of the elderly. Mickey Rooney and Brooke Astor were victims of this.

7. Financial Abuse of Elders Committed by Servants, Repairmen and Contractors

A general rule of thumb with this situation is to have a contract made up prior to the work being started. Perhaps even get it notarized. (Other parts of this book also can be applicable in this category.)

1. Use workmen who are established in the community such that if they rip you off, it could hurt their standing with the community and thus their source of jobs.

2. Check their standing with the Better Business Bureau and even do a background search. You might need to ask him for some information (but not necessarily.) Background searches can be ordered online.

3. Ask for references and investigate them.

4. Look up information online about him/her/them. In MULTIPLE search engines look up their name, and at the same time type in your area/town. Go at least 3 web pages deep into what the search engine presents. Google might not be the best to use for this kind of search as Google may be too mainstream. Angieslist.com is one website to look in. Someone might even have written about them on Facebook.

5. Don't give out too much information to strangers, or initially let people you don't know that well into your home.

6. Are they friendly? This point perhaps holds minor value but if he/she is already nasty, chances are good you'll get more of the same if they're hired.

7. If the worker becomes too inquisitive about your holdings, perhaps tell him you no longer have power of attorney or that you don't own the property.

8. If construction goes over-budget without a prior agreement, perhaps get second opinion(s) and/or put off making the decision about ordering the additional work.

9. Ask ahead of time for receipts for goods bought for the job. If nothing else perhaps you'll need them for tax purposes.

10. Beware of socializing with the workers for too long when they are expecting to work. You could indirectly end up paying for those extra hours of chatting.

11. Does he want cash up-front to first go get supplies? That could be a red flag. He might come back the next day with little or nothing and say prices have gone up and he needs more money.

8. Things you can do to protect your senior citizen family member or friend (not necessarily in order of importance as certain suggestions may be more applicable to your case than others):

1. Read and take seriously the list presented several pages ago as well as other information in this book.

2. Ask the police to do a "well-being check" of the elder if things don't seem right. Just one free visit by the police early on could have saved my family from this disaster. They need to be aware of the potential predator though. Also perhaps contact the NAPSA and anonymously (at least at first) discuss your concerns.

3. Live with him/her, or see him or her often, so you can better monitor his/her activities and contacts.

4. Do not make the mistake of thinking the senior citizen has adequately vetted the potential predator, even if he thinks so. Even though he or she is your elder and speaks with confidence, elders can be wrong. Don't respect his opinion so much that you don't dwell a lot deeper into the potential predator's action, past and present. I write this from experience.

5. Be concerned if he is exploring for the first time, or after a long hiatus, his or her homosexual side, particularly if his or her potential lover is the more aggressive of the two and/or has dominating qualities that his or her spouse had.

6. If you suspect someone may be acting as a predator, have your victim tell them he/she no longer has power of attorney to his/her own estate. Now see how long the potential predator stays in the picture.

7. If dementia (this can include Alzheimer's disease) has entered the picture then be concerned no matter what. Senior citizens with dementia are prime targets for predators.

8. Be suspicious if a new friend hangs around your elder too much and/or has secretive behavior.

9. Perhaps watch him closer if he or she likes to be unusual or unique.

10. Make sure he or she does not give out too much information to strangers, or let people they don't know that well into their homes.

11. This deserves mentioning twice on this list. Even though he or she is your elder and speaks with confidence, they could be wrong, and often are. Don't respect his opinion so much that you don't dwell a lot deeper into the potential predator's action, past and present.

12. At the least talk to him if you see signs of erratic or irresponsible financial activity on the elder's part.

13. At the least talk to him about major mood and behavioral changes of the elder.

14. If he or she is going to be in a senior citizen home, make sure the home, as best as possible, monitors convicted predators and potential predators that like to frequent senior citizen facilities for prey. These predators could be a friend or relative of someone else there.

9. Little Known Things You Can Do To Hopefully Reclaim Lost Revenue

There are lawyers whose specialties include elder-abuse law. This includes lawyers that specialize in defending gay financially abused elders. Police and adult-protection workers can be contacted. See the list of elder abuse organizations further on in this book. This book and contents is not to be confused with legal advice. You likely have other options available to hopefully reclaim some or more of your money. Please also investigate them.

You do need to move fast though!!!

Perhaps going to the media about the event, if they publicize it, could speed up actions related to recovery. Often the police and financial institutions don't want you to go to the media though.

Never give your credit/charge card (or it's information) to someone as if they use it later without authorization the financial institution can distance themselves from responsibility.

Federal Reserve Regulation E

By definition, Federal Reserve Regulation E makes a consumer's bank liable for unauthorized electronic transfers from a consumer's account.
The Electronic Fund Transfer Act (EFTA) (15 USC 1693 et seq.) of 1978 is intended to protect individual consumers engaging in electronic fund transfers (EFTs). EFT services include transfers through automated teller machines, point-of-sale terminals, automated clearinghouse systems, telephone bill-payment plans in which periodic or recurring transfers are contemplated, and remote banking programs.

"Regulation E provides a basic framework that establishes the rights, liabilities, and responsibilities of participants in electronic fund transfer systems such as automated teller machine transfers, telephone bill-payment services, point-of-sale (POS) terminal transfers in stores, and preauthorized transfers from or to a consumer's account (such as direct deposit and social security payments). The term "electronic fund transfer" (EFT) generally refers to a transaction initiated through an electronic terminal, telephone, computer, or magnetic tape that instructs a financial institution either to credit or to debit a consumer's asset account."
(*Reference*: www.federalreserve.gov/bankinforeg/regecg.htm.)

www.federalreserve.gov/boarddocs/supmanual/cch/efta.pdf (pdf file)
www.bargaineering.com/articles/regulation-e-understanding-debit-card-fraud-rules.html
www.federalreserve.gov/bankinforeg/regecg.htm
http://ecfr.gpoaccess.gov/cgi/t/text/textidx?c=ecfr&sid=635f26c4af3e2fe43 27fd25ef4cb5638&tpl=/ecfrbrowse/Title12/12cfr205_main_02.tpl

Federal Reserve Regulation D

www.nacha.org/RulesSimplificationResourcePage
www.fatwallet.com/forums/finance/1023728

TIP: Typically you are significantly more protected when you use a credit card than if using a debit card.

As an example, users of various Lucky's supermarket's self-service checkout counters found that out the hard way from "card skimming" (Thieves had somehow installed equipment into the self-service checkout machinery that would send them the buyer's credit card #s, debit card #s and PINs #s, etc. after they paid for their groceries.)

Those using their debit cards had a much shorter time to report the theft and a larger deductible compared to those using their credit cards. Check with your financial institution to see if you have the same credit card protection if using your debit card. Perhaps you do.

10. Various Elder Abuse Organizations & Related Websites

*National Adult Protective Services Association (NAPSA)
*Consumer Financial Protection Bureau's Office of Older Americans - 1-800-677-1116
*Coalition to End Elder Financial Abuse (CEASE)
*National Committee for the Prevention of Elder Abuse
*Elder Investment Fraud and Financial Exploitation (EIFFE) Prevention Program
*National Center on Elder Abuse
*www.eldercare.gov - Online Elder Care Locator - (Follow appropriate links)
*www.smpresource.org
*National Education and Resource Center on Women and Retirement (Administration on Aging)
*Women's Institute for a Secure Retirement (WISER)
*California Alliance
*MetLife Mature Market Institute
*National Center on Elder Abuse (NCEA)
*The Guardian Project (New York)
*Elder Abuse Prevention Program Institute on Aging
*www.canhr.org/factsheets/abuse_fs/html/fs_financialabuse.htm
*The National Association of State Units on Aging
*Clearinghouse on Abuse and Neglect - Consumer Studies, University of Delaware
*Commission on Law and Aging American Bar Association

END

100 Great Lines To Put in Your Personal Ad

These books are sold and/or distributed with the understanding that the publishers and authors are not engaged in rendering legal or other professional services. **These books and its subject matter are for entertainment purposes only.** In this publication there may be inadvertent inaccuracies including technical inaccuracies, typographical inaccuracies and other possible inaccuracies. **The writers and publishers of these publications expressly disclaim all liability for the use or interpretation by anybody of information contained in these publications.** The authors, publishers and distributors of these publications hereby disclaim any and all liability for any loss or damage caused by errors or omissions resulted from negligence, accident, or any other causes. If legal advice or other expert assistance is required, the services of a competent professional person in a consultation capacity should be sought. Products, services and websites' content vary with time. Please verify any published information.

Copyright (C) 2013

Introduction

The lines in this book can be combined with other lines you may think of to make your personal ad all it can be. Some lines in the book might need adapting to best suit you and/or your sex.

TAGLINES: Your short "tagline" is a headline that, perhaps along with your picture, can get readers to further explore your ad. Great taglines are like gold and people have paid hundreds of dollars for them! Now however many are on the Internet for you to see and use.

Remember, people love to laugh. A funny tagline is a big plus.

There is a great deal of material in this book to build quality taglines from. You may also want to take a bit of time and do a web search for "best personal ad taglines" for ideas. Chances are others (including those looking at your ad) haven't seen the tagline already, or have forgotten it if they did.

This book however is the best collection of personal ad lines that I'm aware of online or offline.

The Lines

It's suggested that you combine a healthy number of lines with specific information about yourself. Most of the lines below can be combined with each other so mix and match as you see fit!

A day not in love is a lost opportunity.

My friends know me as spontaneous, spritely, and upbeat.

I am searching for a beautiful person inside and out.

Are you looking for real love and someone special?

I enjoy thought provoking dialogue.

Together let's seek our destiny.

I hope only to fulfill your every desire.

I love making people happy and to see them smile, even if at times it is at my own expense.

I feel the most pleasure when I know I am doing/enduring something to please another.

I'm looking to learn, not just to play....

I'd like to explore hidden fantasies with you.

I want to be taken to that special place and beyond.

I have the financial and emotional capacity to take care of myself.

Unlike perhaps others here I'm not misrepresenting myself. I know the importance of honesty.

I love sex. Rough sex, fun sex, emotional sex... I want you to respect me before and after but during is negotiable.

I want to explore my naughty side,

I'm looking for a friend, confidant and lover.

Like me I'd like you to be thoughtful, attractive, and looking to expand yourself as a person.

I have developed intricate pleasure techniques which can slowly arouse and pleasure beyond imagination.

I think I would describe myself, briefly, as quite a sociable person with a good sense of humor who doesn't take herself too seriously...having said that I believe I am also thoughtful and caring and someone who places great value on good friendships and relationships.

I am loyal, compassionate and respectful of people and animals. People describe me as easy going and good natured.

I have got great plans and goals in my life which I want to achieve.

I'm a contemporary yet spiritual soul in search of his charming, compassionate and caring companion to share this journey of life.

Are you looking for someone to grow with and push things further?

I have a wise mind and younger spirit.

I am an easy going, and loyal friend.

I'm looking forward to a fantastic voyage of a relationship.
I am attracted to someone who enjoys learning and growing.

Are you looking for fun, adventure and a challenge? If so I'm your girl.

I'm a passionate person with interests numerous and diverse.

I am trustworthy, affectionate, passionate, loving and non-judgmental. I am happy with myself and my accomplishments.

I want someone kind, loving, honest, communicative and self-aware. Your developed interest in education, hygiene, aesthetics, style and emotional literacy would make life easier for us. I'd like to find someone interested in building a relationship based on an accomplished life and a win/win attitude.

I am looking for someone who can work themselves deep inside my mind and make me fall to my knees.

Are you looking for someone to make you happy...someone that won't just have sex with you but will make love to you?

We all want to achieve heart pounding serenity.

I am looking for something more than just sex and games. Sure sex is a part of it but I also want someone that I can spend time with. I want the total package. I want someone that I can go out with, talk with, laugh with, and fall in love with.

Outside of our playtime, I'd like to enjoy a harmony that can grow into a loving, trusting relationship. I enjoy the outdoors and staying healthy, going out on the town from time to time and hanging out at home.

My last relationship ended because we grew in different directions.

I am usually lucky and love life. I would like to find someone like that.

I'm a strong, seductive, passionate woman who is established and knows herself.

I'm well educated and well-travelled. I'm gainfully employed and very independent. I enjoy traveling, good food and wine, the theater and sports.

I'm searching for an open minded man with an adventurous soul and sensual heart. A journey in love is the destination. We still have plenty of time but none to waste! A beautiful world is waiting. Let's enjoy while we can!

I'll laugh at your corny jokes.

I'm a writer and voracious reader. I'm smart, and I like smart people.

Physical attraction leads to animal instincts.

I have a strong passion for the exploration and power of touch in all its forms.

I enjoy knowledge, I like to learn new and exciting things.

I am cosmopolitan and highly educated. I am a baby boomer, in good shape and would like an agemate and a partner who understands mutuality. I am interested in developing a long term relationship.

I am interested in meeting someone who is honest, open and enjoys (his)her kink.

I have very many interests and I'm passionate about all of them! I love movies, literature, music, art, theatre, science… and lots of other things.

I am fun, open-minded, spontaneous and down for raunchy action.

The reason openness is important to me is that it shows that someone accepts themselves.

I'm lively and active and have a well developed sense of humor.

I hope to always be me and take advantage of any opportunities and chances whenever they're thrown at me.

I am totally devoted when in love.

I'm a laid-back, drama-free kind of person.

I want to be late to my own funeral.

Physical play is quite enjoyable but chemistry and a connection is more important.

I like to laugh, I like to have fun.

I believe that love is not what we see but what we do.

I won't ignore you or abandon you. I'm not looking for a secondary relationship.

I have a well developed and dominant sexual identity. I am seeking a man who is a smart, uninhibited, challenging partner.

I consider myself a natural leader, an innovator, a creator. I fight for the best and readily take the risks incumbent with leading a fulfilled, enriched life.

I am a strong, confident thinker, with a secure sense of himself (herself).

I consider myself to be a spontaneous, fun loving person. I work hard, play hard, and enjoy life. I'm a very affectionate and passionate. I like to hold hands and believe it or not cuddle. I believe in treating others the way I would like to be treated. I am looking for someone to grow with spiritually, mentally and physically. I want someone who is not afraid to love and be loved, someone who is affectionate, passionate and good kisser.

I will love you and take good care of you. I am someone who you can trust and believe in, someone who will always want to make you feel happy.

I'm neat and clean both internally and externally.

I want true love and real commitment.

I am looking for something more than just sex and games. There is a balance that is needed since none of us can live in a purely sexual world. Sure sex is an important part of it all but I also want someone that I can spend time with. I want the total package. I want someone I can go out with, talk with, laugh with, and fall in love with.

I want something that will naturally grow and evolve into its own very beautiful story.

I enjoy a great number of things and am very open to experimentation.

I'm interested in your fantasies.

I want to touch your body, your soul, your life.

I still believe that fairytales can come true, it can happen to us...

I live a healthy lifestyle. I am seeking the same.

I am brimming with sexual desire.

I will be looking forward to hear from you and Your wish will always be done...

I am looking for a partner - but I am happy to form a friendship.

Living on earth is expensive...but it does include free trips around the sun.

I eat healthy and workout regularly.

I am an educated, intelligent professional with eclectic tastes in most everything: art, music, food, people, entertainment and travel.

I'm looking for a non-smoker to share my life with in all ways, a friend and companion to travel with, commiserate over bad days and rejoice over good days; a lover and confidant.

Educated, professional and kinky.

I have class and style. I know the value of dressing to impress.

I would love to be able to say "I've finally found you."

I believe that we all have the ability to create or change anything.

I consider myself to be a sharp, crafty, inventive, fun, strong woman who enjoys life more when she's in a relationship.

I'm looking for a like minded man to chat, debate and play with.

I'm not a just fantasist wasting your time.

I am people biased not gender biased.

I am family-oriented and have family values.

I possess confidence but take pride in not being arrogant. I'm persistent but respectful. I have intelligence and charm.

I don't like negative people. We're here to live life not fear it.

I have learned in life that the smallest good deed is better than the grandest good intention.

I have high hopes for us.

I am a sharp, crafty, inventive, fun woman who doesn't hate men or hate anyone for that matter.

I enjoy life so much more when I'm in a relationship.

What you are like OUT of bed makes you more desirable for me to want you to take me there.

I like to please as much as be pleased.

I want to discover and explore my limits as well as push them further.

I like intellectual conversations.

My ambition is self-actualisation, to release the potential within.

I'm thoughtful, devoted, industrious, competitive, genuine and trustworthy.

I'm looking to learn and grow, not just to play....